NEURAL NETWORK TRAINING USING GENETIC ALGORITHMS

SERIES IN MACHINE PERCEPTION AND ARTIFICIAL INTELLIGENCE*

Editors: **H. Bunke** (Univ. Bern, Switzerland)
P. S. P. Wang (Northeastern Univ., USA)

*For the complete list of titles in this series, please write to the Publisher.

NEURAL NETWORK TRAINING USING GENETIC ALGORITHMS

A J F van Rooij
Twente University of Technology

L C Jain
University of South Australia

R P Johnson
Australian Defence Sci.Tech. Organisation

World Scientific
Singapore • New Jersey • London • Hong Kong

Published by

World Scientific Publishing Co. Pte. Ltd.

P O Box 128, Farrer Road, Singapore 912805

USA office: Suite 1B, 1060 Main Street, River Edge, NJ 07661

UK office: 57 Shelton Street, Covent Garden, London WC2H 9HE

British Library Cataloguing-in-Publication Data
A catalogue record for this book is available from the British Library.

First published 1996
First repint 1998

ISBN 981-02-2919-4

Printed in Singapore.

Preface

The tremendous interest in the intelligent techniques, including artificial neural networks, genetic algorithms and fuzzy logic, has paved the way for the development of hybrid techniques such as a combination of neural networks and genetic algorithms to solve industrial problems. This book investigates the possibility of using genetic algorithms in the final stage of the design of a neural classifier system, which serves to classify various sets of input data into their respective classes. In this stage, a feed-forward neural network with a fixed architecture is trained to perform this classification. Presently, most neural networks of this type are trained using a steepest descent learning algorithm, usually referred to as the back-propagation algorithm. Since genetic algorithms are, at least in theory, inherently able to find good solutions for most optimisation problems, this technique is investigated in this book as to their performance and viability in the field of neural network weight optimisation.

This book contains six chapters. Chapter one gives an introduction to artificial neural networks. Chapter two describes the genetic algorithms, and its biological counterpart. After this introduction of genetic algorithms, a more comprehensive mathematical basis for their functioning and characteristics is provided in chapter three. In chapter four a special genetic algorithm is designed and optimised for the sole use of training neural networks, based on neural network characteristics and GA-specific theories on crossover disruption and the hitch-hiker phenomenon. Subsequently, several case-studies are performed, using problems of various sizes and complexity. The results of these case-studies are presented in chapter five. The results are interpreted and discussed thoroughly in order to give a better understanding of the mechanics at work. In chapter six the same problems are solved using the normal back-propagation learning algorithm, which is presently mostly used for neural network learning. This chapter serves to present our recent results of neural network training using genetic algorithms in a broader perspective. Finally, a list containing references and further reading is included, as well as an index at the end of this book.

This book will be useful for application engineers, scientists, researchers and the senior undergraduate/first year graduate students in Computer, Electrical, Electronic, Manufacturing, Mechatronics and Mechanical Engineering, and related disciplines.

We would like to thank the Australian Defence Science and Technology Organisation for supporting this research (contract number 332557).

Arno van Rooij wishes to thank Michelle Osborne for her support during the preparation of this book.

Finally, we would like to thank Prof. Dr. H. Bunke for the opportunity to publish this book.

Arno van Rooij
Lakhmi Jain
Ray Johnson

Table of Contents

1. Artificial Neural Networks

Artificial neural networks are parallel computational models comprised of densely interconnected adaptive processing units [Jain, 1995]. These networks are fine-grained parallel implementations of non-linear systems, either static or dynamic. A very important feature of these networks is their adaptive nature where 'learning by example' replaces 'programming' in solving problems. This feature renders these computational models very appealing in application domains, where one has little or incomplete understanding of the problem to be solved, but where training data (examples) are available. Another key feature is the intrinsic parallel architecture that allows for fast computation of solutions when these networks are implemented on parallel digital computers or when implemented in customised hardware.

Artificial neural networks are viable and very important computational models for a wide variety of problems. These include pattern classification, speech synthesis and recognition, function approximation, image compression, associative memory, clustering, forecasting and prediction, combinatorial optimisation, and non-linear system modeling and control. The networks are 'neural' in the sense that they have been inspired by neuroscience, the study of the human brain and nervous system. The artificial neurons used are thought to be very simple models of their biological counterpart. However, this does not mean that they are faithful models of biological neural or cognitive phenomena, those are of a much more complex nature. In fact, the majority of the neural networks presently used are more closely related to traditional mathematical and/or statistical models, such as non-parametric pattern classifiers, non-linear filters and statistical regression models, than they do to neurobiological models. Still, the technology of neural networks attempts to mimic nature's approach to solve certain complex problems that are impossible to solve with the more traditional techniques.

1.1   Introduction

This section introduces some of the basic aspects of neural networks. The basic components of neural networks are discussed and some of the more common forms of neural networks are considered.

The study of neural networks was commenced as an attempt to understand the behaviour and structure of the biological neuron. It was soon realised how inadequate the artificial neuron models were in comparison with the biological neuron. As a result some researchers in artificial neural networks decided that the name of neuron was inappropriate and used other terms such as node rather than neuron. The use of the term neuron is now so deeply entrenched that its continued general use seems assured.

Another point which is sometimes confusing is that different writers use a different numbering nomenclature for multi-layered neural networks. Some workers do not count the input layer as one of the layers on the basis that this layer often serves only for the input data and no processing of data occurs in it. Processing however does occur within the input layer in some forms of artificial neural network. For the sake of consistency it seems desirable to include the input layer as one of the layers when numbering the layers of neurons.

The artificial neuron

The artificial neuron (refer figure 1.1) may be thought of as an attempt to model the behaviour of the biological neuron. It is at the present time a fairly rough approximation to the behaviour of a biological neuron and it is probably not desirable to stretch the analogy too far.

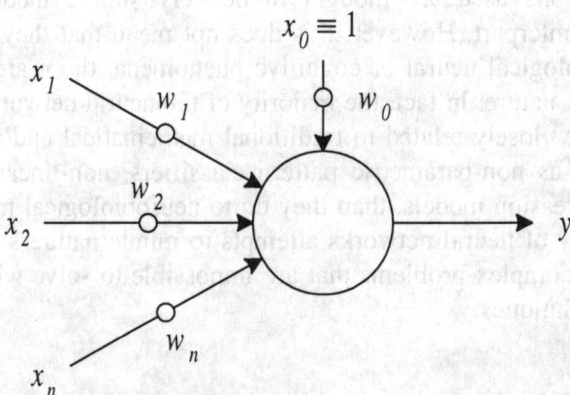

Figure 1.1   *The artificial neuron*

The first stage is a process where the inputs x_0, x_1, ... x_n multiplied by their respective weights w_0, w_1, ... w_n are summed by the neuron.. The input vector x_0, x_1, ... x_n may be denoted by X and the weight vector w_0, w_1, ... w_n by W. Weight w_0 forms the neuron's threshold. A dummy input x_0, which is always equal to 1, is used for this. The resulting summation process may be shown as:

$$y = w_0 + x_1 \cdot w_1 + x_2 \cdot w_2 + \dots + x_n \cdot w_n$$

$$= X \cdot W$$

The input vector X is comprised of the inputs to the neuron $x_0, x_1, \dots x_n$. The inputs contain various kinds of information depending on the system being studied by the neural network.

The weight vector W contains the *weights* connecting the various parts of the network. The memory of the neural network is stored in the values of the weights. The term weight is used in neural network terminology and is a means of expressing of the strength of the connection between any two neurons in the neural network.

During training phase of a neural network the values of the weights are continuously modified by the training process until some previously agreed criteria are met. Different types of network use different methods of making the necessary adjustments.

The perceptron

In order to allow for varying input conditions and their effect on the output it is usually necessary to include an *activation function f* in the neuron arrangement. This is so that adequate levels of amplification may be used where necessary for small input signals without running the risk of driving the output to unacceptable limits where a large input signal is applied. Depending on the circumstances one of a number of different activation functions are employed. Figure 1.2 shows a simplified representation of a perceptron.

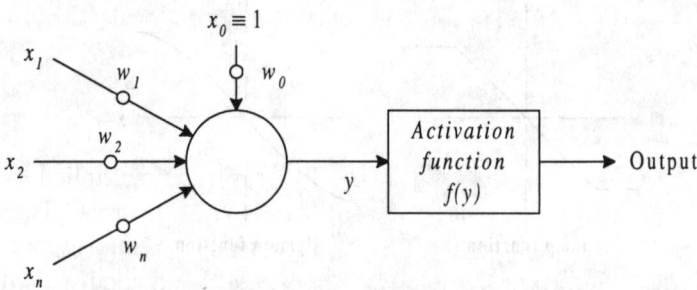

Figure 1.2   *The perceptron*

The output of the neuron is now expressed in the form

Output $= f(y)$

Activation functions

There are a number of types of commonly used activation functions and some of these are shown in figure 1.3. Most activation functions are also known as *threshold functions* or *squashing functions*. A brief description of the properties of the activation functions shown in figure 1.3 follows:

- Step function. The function shown in figure 1.3a is known as the step function. The output from this function is limited to one of two values, depending on whether the input signal is greater or less than zero. Usually the output value would be one for signal values greater than zero and minus one for signal values les than zero That is:

$$Output = 1 \quad \text{when} \quad y > 0$$
$$= -1 \qquad \qquad y < 0$$

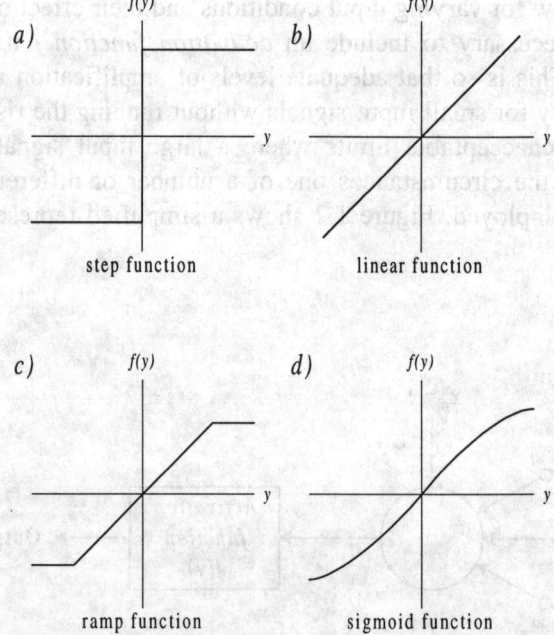

Figure 1.3   *Some common types of activation functions*

- Linear function. The linear function is shown in figure 1.3b and this is the only linear function in the group of four functions shown. The effect of this function is to multiply by a constant factor. That is:

$$\text{Output} = K \cdot y$$

- Ramp function. The effect of the ramp function, shown in figure 1.3c, is to behave as a linear function between the upper and lower limits and once these limits are reached to then behave as a step function. Under some circumstances this feature of providing a linear output between defined limits can be of value. Another attraction is that the function may be simply defined:

$$
\begin{aligned}
\text{Output} &= \text{Max} & &\text{when } y > \text{upper limit} \\
&= K \cdot y & &y < \text{upper limit and } y > \text{lower limit} \\
&= \text{Min} & &y < \text{lower limit}
\end{aligned}
$$

- Sigmoid function. The sigmoid function is an 'S' shaped curve, as shown in figure 1.3d. A number of mathematical expressions may be used to define an 'S' shaped curve, but the most commonly used form is given by the expression:

$$f(y) = \frac{1}{1 + e^{-y}}$$

This expression is easy to differentiate and sometimes this property enables a simplification to be made in the neural network formulation.

Two layer neural network

Several perceptrons of the above form may then be grouped together to form a neural network where the two layers of neurons are fully interconnected, but there is no interconnection between neurons in the same layer. This results in a network as shown in figure 1.4. This arrangement is a two layer neural network and it illustrates a common form of neural networks.

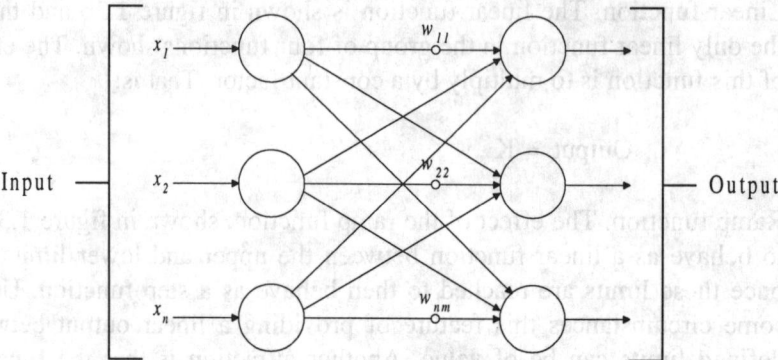

Figure 1.4   *Two layer fully interconnected neural network*

Types of neural network

Neural networks may be classified in a number of different ways depending on their underlying principles of operation. An indication of the methods of classification is given in the table 1.1 below. Many different types of neural networks have been developed, but only a limited number will be discussed. The various types of learning and recall will be explained in the following sections.

Table 1.1   *Classification of neural networks*

	Feedback Recall	**Feed-forward Recall**
Unsupervised Learning	Type A Example: Adaptive Resonance Theorem	Type B Example: Linear Associative Memory
Supervised Learning	Type C Example: Brain State in Box	Type D Example: Perceptron

Learning

Before a neural network can be used it is necessary to subject it some form of training during which process the values of the weights in the network are adjusted to reflect the characteristics of the input data. The learning process is one of developing a mapping between the output data and the input data. When the network is adequately trained, it will retrieve the correct output when a set of input data is presented to it. A valuable property of a neural network is that of generalisation. Generalisation is the ability of a trained neural network to provide a correct matching of output data to a set of previously unseen input data.

In training a network the available input dataset consists of many facts and is randomly divided into two groups. One group of facts is used as the training data and a second group is retained for checking and testing the accuracy of the performance of the network after training. The quantity of data available should be large enough to encompass a representative range of circumstances which the network will encounter during service.

As indicated in table 1.1 there are two forms of learning: *supervised learning* and *unsupervised learning*.

- **Supervised learning.**
In this form of learning, a target value is included as part of each fact within the training data. In this instance a fact incorporates all of the input data for the particular event and the required output expected from the network for this fact. The target value is the output value corresponding to a particular fact.

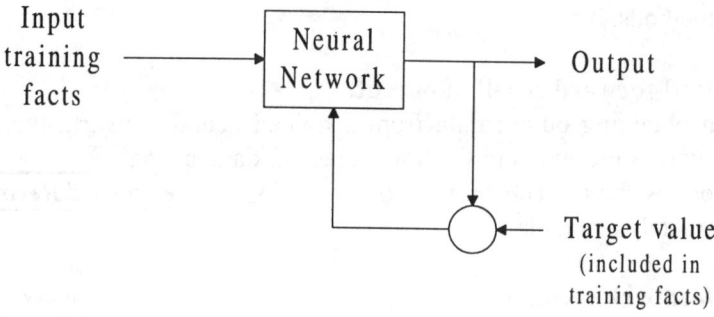

Figure 1.5   *Example of supervised learning in a neural network*

During the training process, the set of training data facts is repeatedly applied to the network until the difference between the output results and the target values are within the desired tolerance. When the neural network meets the error limits using the training facts the previously unseen test data set of facts is applied to the neural network. This tests the generalisation performance of the network.

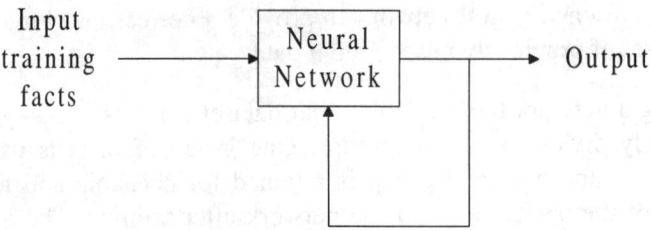

Figure 1.6 *Example of unsupervised learning in a neural network*

- **Unsupervised learning.**
Unlike supervised learning there is no target value in this form of training. Instead, the set of data which contains the facts is repeatedly applied to the network until a stable network output is obtained. It has been suggested that this form of training is more similar to the biological neuron as in the biological situation there is not normally a target value.

Recall of output data from the trained network

The recall of output from a trained neural network is obtained by two distinct methods.

- **The feed-forward recall of output.**
When obtaining output data from a trained neural network, the novel input data is presented to the trained network and a single traverse of the network is made. The output corresponding to the input data is then immediately available.

- **The feedback recall of output.**
In this case, the applied input data is circulated in the trained neural network until a stable condition is obtained. This is intrinsically a more lengthy process than the corresponding feed-forward recall of data.

Learning rules

There are a large number of training rules that have been developed and some are listed below. The role of the learning mechanism is to adjust the weights of the network in response to the poblem.

Table 1.2   *Indicative arrangements of some important types of learning rules*

Rule	Weight Adjustment Δw_{ij}	Comments
Hebbian (nearly all network training theories are some variant of Hebbs rule)	$\Delta w_{ij} = \eta f(w_i X) x_j$	η = learning rate w = weight vector X = input vector
Perceptron (binary response, no action if no error)	$\Delta w_{ij} = \eta (t_i - sgn(w_i X)) x_j$	t = target vector η = learning rate
Delta	$\Delta w_{ji} = \eta\, \delta_{pj} a_{pi}$ A: $\delta_{pj} = f'(S_j)(t_{pj} - a_{pj})$ B: $\delta_{pj} = f'(S_j)\Sigma_k \delta_k w_{kj}$	S_j = weighted sum of inputs to j A: output layer error B: hidden layer error
Least Mean Square (Widrow-Hoff)	$\Delta w_i = \eta (t_i - w_i X) x_j$	η, t, X and w are as above
Outstar (Grossberg)	$\Delta w_{ji} = \eta (t_i - w_{ji})$	
Winner Takes All (nearby neurons modify in a similar fashion)	A: $\Delta w_{ij} = \eta (x_j - w_{ij})$ B: $\Delta w_{ij} = 0$	A: when in near neighbourhood B: when not in near neighbourhood

Forms of neural network connections

Neurons may be arranged in many different ways, from the relatively uncomplicated fully interconnected layer (figure 1.7), to more complicated arrangements such as multi-layer networks (figure 1.8)., through to for example the Adaptive Resonance Theory networks. Some simple examples of possible forms of network connections are given in the following figures.

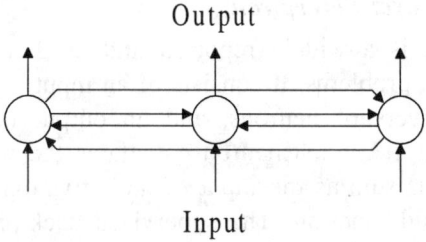

Output

Input

Figure 1.7   *Fully interconnected layer*

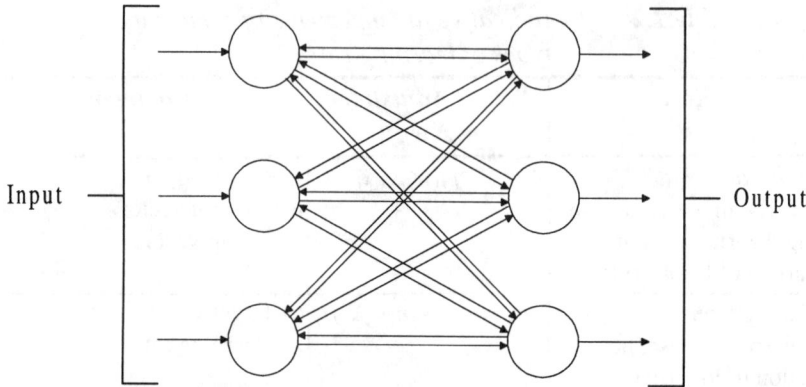

Figure 1.8   *Two layer recurrent network
(note the feedback connections)*

1.2   Basic types of neural networks

A number of neural networks are successfully used and reported in literature. Some common examples of different types of networks are:

- Perceptron network
- Multiple Layer Perceptron (MLP)
- Radial Basis Function network
- Kohonen's self organising feature map
- Adaptive Resonance Theory network (ART)
- Hopfield network
- Bidirectional Associative Memory (BAM) network
- Counter-propagation network
- Cognitron & neo-cognitron network

Some of these networks will be described in further detail.

The Multiple Layer Perceptron

The MLP network is a widely reported and used neural network in a number of practical problems. It consists of an input layer of neurons, one or more hidden layers of neurons, and an output layer of neurons as illustrated in figure 1.9. Each neuron calculates the weighted sum of its inputs, and uses this sum as the input of an activation function, which is commonly a sigmoid function. The supervised back-propagation learning algorithm, uses gradient descent search in the weight space to minimise the error between the target output and the actual output. A large number of

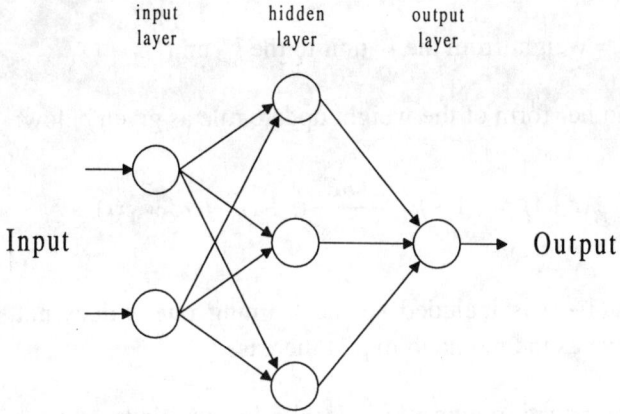

input layer   hidden layer   output layer

Input   Output

Figure 1.9   *A typical Multiple Layer Perceptron (MLP) architecture*

gradient-based search methods are reported in the literature. The back-propagation method is chosen due to its popularity.

The mean squared error, often called *training error* or *network error*, between the actual output and the desired output is defined as follows:

$$E = \frac{1}{2}\sum_k (t_k - y_k)^2 \tag{1.1}$$

where

$\quad t_k$ = target output of the kth neuron in the output layer
$\quad y_k$ = actual output of the kth neuron in the output layer

The derivative of the error, with respect to each weight is set proportional to weight change as:

$$\Delta w_{jk} = -\varepsilon \cdot \frac{\partial E}{\partial w_{jk}} \tag{1.2}$$

where ε is called the *learning rate*.

It is a general practice to accelerate the learning procedure by introducing a momentum term μ into the learning equation (1.2), as follows:

$$\Delta w_{jk}(t+1) = -\varepsilon \cdot \frac{\partial E}{\partial w_{jk}}(t+1) + \mu \cdot \Delta w_{jk}(t) \tag{1.3}$$

where

w_{jk} = weight from the jth unit to the kth unit

There is another form of the weight update rule as given below:

$$\Delta w_{jk}(t+1) = -(1-\mu)\varepsilon \cdot \frac{\partial E}{\partial w_{jk}}(t+1) + \mu \cdot \Delta w_{jk}(t) \tag{1.4}$$

The factor $(1-\mu)$ is included so the learning rate ε does not need to be stepped down as the momentum μ is increased.

The back-propagation algorithm, despite its simplicity and popularity, has several drawbacks. It is slow and typically needs thousands of iterations to train a network to solve a simple problem. The algorithm is also dependent on the initial weights, and the values of μ and ε.

The Radial Basis Function (RBF) network

The Radial Basis Function network consists of three layers. The hidden layer is used to cluster inputs of the network; neurons in this layer are therefore called cluster centres. Though its architecture is similar to a three layer back-propagation network, its operation is different. It uses Gaussian kernel functions to calculate the activations of the neurons in the first layer. The neurons in the output layer perform an ordinary linear weighted sum of these activations. Learning in this network is in two stages. First, the input training patters are clustered (unsupervised) to their nearest cluster centres by means of a clustering algorithm. After this, the spread of each function about its cluster centre is determined. For example, the function widths can be made equal to the average distance between the cluster centre and the training patterns clustered with that centre, or they can be set equal to the average distance between the cluster centre and its nearest cluster centres (often two).

The second stage of learning is the supervised learning of the weights of the output layer which associates the basis function outputs with specific classes.

The performance of the Radial Basis Function network depends on the way the inputs are clustered. As with the back-propagation network, the number of neurons in the hidden layer greatly influences the performance of the network. The training time of this network is typically orders of magnitude smaller than that for the back-propagation network, as training is split up in two parts, both of which can be quite fast.

Kohonen's self organising feature map

The Kohonen self organising feature map has two layers of neurons. The signals from input neurons are fed to every neuron in the feature map. While learning (unsupervised) the network generates a two dimensional representation of the input space. The multi-dimensional input space is transferred to a two-dimensional grid using this network. Figure 1.10 shows a Kohonen network that has two inputs and a grid (or feature map) consisting of 3 by 3 = 9 neurons.

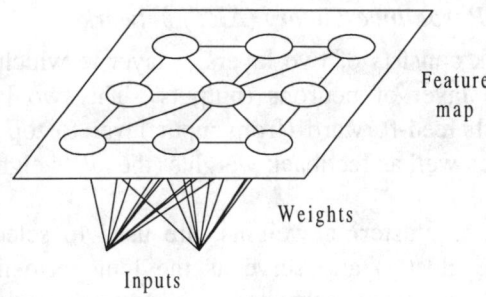

Figure 1.10   *A '2-3-3' 2-dimensional Kohonen network*

Learning in the Kohonen network is performed using competition in the feature map that results in a dominant winning neuron for a certain training input. This neuron has the weights that most closely resemble the values of the inputs. The weights of this neuron as well as of its neighbours are then updated to more closely resemble the input vector. The neighbours are determined by a neighbourhood function. The radius of this neighbourhood function describes how many neurons around the winning neuron are included in the neighbourhood. There are several shapes possible for this function. A square shape, a bubble (circle) shape or a hexagonal shape are most commonly used.

In order to train the network properly, both the learning rate and the radius of the neighbourhood function should decrease in time. The initial weights of the network should be different from each other and are often set to random values in the range of the possible input values.

The learning process consists of two phases. In the first phase, coarse learning, the learning rate is quite large and the neighbourhood radius decreases from encompassing a large part of the grid to encompassing only the winning neuron itself (radius = 0) or the winning neuron and its closest neighbours (radius = 1). In the second phase, the learning rate slowly decreases to zero (this is usually the stopping criterion) while the neighbourhood radius remains 0 or 1.

The learning rate as well as the neighbourhood radius can decrease by a number of functions, e.g. linearly or exponential. The total number of training steps (this is the number of times a single input training pattern is presented to the network) is typically 500 times the number of network units or less, with the first phase of learning lasting only about 1000 cycles.

The Adaptive Resonance Theory (ART) network

The ART1 network consists of two layers; a layer to which the inputs are applied and a top layer of neurons (outputs). The two layers are fully interconnected with feed-forward (from input layer to top layer) weights (the 'W' weights) as well as feedback weights (the 'V' weights).

The 'W' weights, or clustering weights, are used to select the winning output neuron (the cluster) and serve as the long term memory of the network. The winning neuron is the neuron with the maximum response (= weighted sum) for a certain input pattern applied to the winner-take-all competitive output layer. The 'V' weights, or vigilance weights, are used for the vigilance test and serve as the short term memory of the network. When a training pattern is similar enough to the last pattern clustered with the winning neuron, it will be clustered with this neuron. Otherwise, the neuron with the second largest response is tried. The required similarity is determined by the vigilance threshold. If the input does not cluster with any of the existing clusters (output neurons), then a new cluster centre is made. The vigilance threshold (between 0 and 1) determines how similar two patterns should be before they are clustered together. The larger the threshold, the less patterns are clustered together and therefore the more clusters will be made. When an input pattern is clustered with an existing or a new cluster centre, its weights are updated. The 'V' weights are set equal to this input vector and the 'W' weights are set to the normalised input vector. While learning this way, the network works as a 'follow the leader' system.

Testing or recall of ART1 is performed by feeding a pattern into the input layer and selecting the neuron with maximum response (the winning neuron) using the feed-forward weights. The output of the network (i.e. the winning neuron) is the one whose weights are most similar (the smallest Hamming distance) to the input (test) pattern.

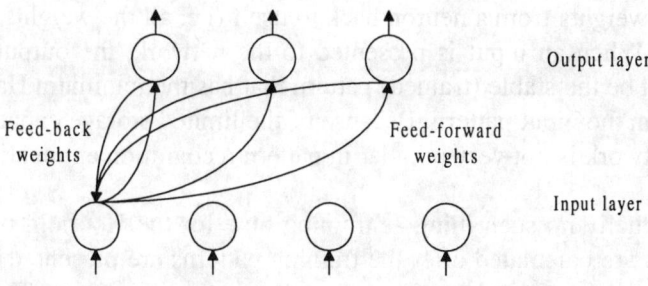

Figure 1.11 *A '4-3' ART1 network*

Figure 1.11 shows an ART1 network with 4 inputs and 3 output neurons (clusters); a '4-3' network. Only the weights for one neuron are shown in the figure.

The ART1 network can only be used for binary input values. Other versions of the algorithm exists, for example ART2, that can handle continuous valued inputs.

The Hopfield network

The Hopfield network is a fully connected single layer network. After an input pattern is presented to the network, it will converge by means of a state update rule until it resides in a stable pattern. The state of a neuron is simply its activation ($+1$ or -1), and the starting state of the network is the input. The network can only handle bipolar inputs, or binary inputs with a slightly altered update rule. This is the test or recall procedure. The learning or storing is done simply by setting the weights in the network according to $w_{ij} = s_i \cdot s_j$, where w_{ij} is the weights between neurons i and j, and s_i and s_j are the inputs of neurons i and j. Figure 1.12 shows a 3-neuron Hopfield network.

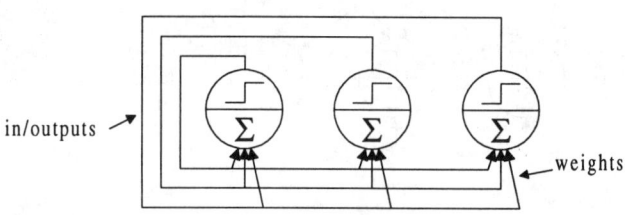

Figure 1.12 *A 3-neuron Hopfield network*

Usually the weights from a neuron back to itself (i.e. all the weights w_{ii}) are set to zero. When an input is presented to the network, the output of the network will be the stable (trained) pattern that has the minimum Hamming distance from the input pattern. Because of the limited storage capacity, the Hopfield network is not very popular in pattern recognition applications.

There is virtually no such thing as training time for the Hopfield network. The weights are calculated after the training patterns are presented and are set to their appropriate values. There is no updating of weights. The recall phase does take time because the network has to undergo several convergence steps before the network has found its stable state.

The Bidirectional Associative Memory (BAM) network

The Bidirectional Associative Memory is quite similar to the Hopfield network. This type of network has two layers of neurons, which are fully interconnected. In the recall phase, an input (test) pattern is presented to one of the two layers. After the recall (test) phase, the network has come to a stable state so that each of the two layers has a stable pattern as output. The updating of the states of the neurons ($-1/+1$) is done for the two layers alternatively, which means that there is a bidirectional data flow while the network is converging.

The storage (learning) procedure is similar to the Hopfield network, except that the BAM network needs inputs to both layers. Figure 1.13 shows a BAM network which as a layer of three neurons (layer A) and a layer of two neurons (layer B).

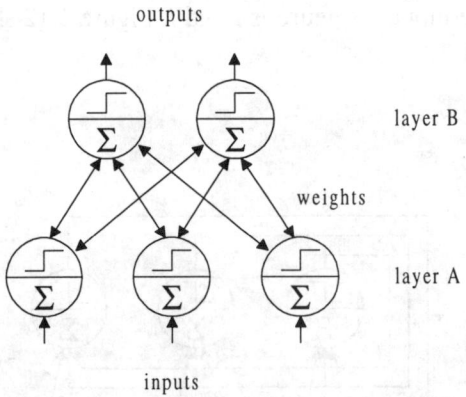

Figure 1.13   *A '3–2' Bidirectional Associative Memory*

For the BAM network, like the Hopfield network, the storage capacity is probably its main limitation. It follows that an optimistic value of the maximum storage capacity is Min(m,n), where m and n are the number of neurons in each of the layers. Thus at the most the smallest of m and n patterns can be stored in the network. A more conservative value is $\sqrt{\text{Min}(m,n)}$.

1.3   Conclusion

Artificial neural networks are viable and important computational models for a wide variety of problems. It is a common practice to use trial and error to find a suitable neural network architecture for a given problem. This trial and error method is not only time consuming, but it may not generate an optimum neural network structure.

The learning process whereby the network encodes information from the training process is also of great importance in neural network implementation.

A number of learning techniques, such as error back-propagation, have been proposed to train neural networks, but all are highly dependent on the interconnection topology. This work reports an effort to develop a more general artificial neural network training technique, based on genetic algorithms, that can be applied to a variety of topologies, possibly allowing new artificial neural network structures to be investigated.

2. Genetic Algorithms

This chapter introduces genetic algorithms, which will be investigated and used to optimise the weights of neural networks. Genetic algorithms (GAs) are part of a collection of stochastic optimisation algorithms, loosely based on the concepts of biological evolutionary theory. These techniques are successfully used in many applications, including the optimisation of neural networks. Since practically all ideas and certainly most of the nomenclature in the field of genetic algorithms are taken from biology, a brief introduction to genetics is presented first, including an overview of the main concepts of Darwinian evolutionary theory. With this biological background, the step to its mathematical counterparts, the genetic algorithms, turns out to be quite logical. It also helps in understanding the fundamentals of the mathematical process related to genetic algorithms.

2.1 Biological background

In living cells, the information that determines their function is carried in pairs of *chromosomes*. A position on such a pair of chromosomes is called a *locus*, which can be thought of as a box containing that information. A locus holds two *genes* (one gene on each chromosome). Genes are therefore the structures from which a chromosome is made up. There is a multitude of different sets of genes, each of them specific to one locus. The set of genes which relate to a specific locus are called *alleles*. A locus can only contain two of these genes, and thus can choose two out of the possible set of alleles (a_1, a_2, ..., a_k). All cells in an organism are identical in their chromosomal content, with certain other factors determining what function a particular cell in an organism performs (e.g. whether a cell functions as a brain cell or as a skin cell).

- **Genotype versus phenotype**

A *genotype* of an individual at a single locus is the pair of genes contained in it. The complete genotype of an individual, or the total genetic package, is the set of all genotypes over all loci, or the totality of all chromosomes. This is also known as the *genome* of an organism. What is actually observed is the *phenotype* and it is formed by the interaction of a genotype with its environment. Different genotypes may therefore result in the same phenotype, or in contrast equal genotypes can result in different phenotypes.

- **Dominant and recessive genes**

In the case of two possible alleles a_1 and a_2 for a single locus, one is often a *dominant* and the other a *recessive* gene. The dominant gene is always expressed in the phenotype, the recessive gene only in the absence of the dominant one. If for instance a_1 is dominant, then with the genotypes a_1a_1, a_1a_2 and a_2a_1 this allele will be expressed in the phenotype, whereas the recessive gene a_2 will only be expressed in the phenotype if the genotype is a_2a_2.

- **Epistasis**

The way a gene is expressed in the phenotype, or whether it is expressed at all, often depends on the presence or absence of one or more other genes. Such an interaction between genes in the expression of the genotype is called *epistasis*. The most common form of epistasis is the *masking effect*, where a single gene can 'turn on' or 'off' the expression in the phenotype of one or more other genes.

Reproduction

In organisms there are two reproductive methods by which cells divide to form new cells. The first kind is *mitosis*, where the parent cell simply divides itself into two cells, identical to the parent cell. This is the main method by which organisms produce new cells in order to grow larger, and is also part of the *asexual reproduction* of simple organisms in relatively stable environments. Asexual reproduction works well in producing generations of offspring that are very similar to their ancestors, but when the environment changes, such an organism has limited ability to adapt and survive.

The second kind, *meiosis*, is used for *sexual reproduction* of two organisms. Major evolutionary change can only occur when there is a large store of genetic variability available. This is usually the case for sexually reproducing organisms. In the process of meiosis, each organism produces *gametes*, which carry half the amount of chromosomes of a normal cell. Each gene has a 50% chance of ending up at the locus at a gamete (although certain genes can be 'linked' within a chromosome, remaining together as a group). The second step of sexual reproduction is fertilisation, where the gametes of the male and the female unite to form one new cell, restoring the original amount of chromosomes and again having two genes at each locus.

Mutations

In the mitosis and meiosis processes, although rare, *mutations* may occur. A mutation is a change in a chromosome that may result in a change in the characteristic of a cell or an organism. A mutated individual is called a mutant. Most often mutations are harmful to the cell or organism, resulting in disease or even death. When they are beneficial however, they provide a basis for variation between and within a species. This ensures the species can improve and/or adapt to changing environments. Mutations can be divided into *chromosome mutations* and *gene mutations*.

One form of chromosome mutation that occurs during meiosis is *recombination*. In this process, the homologous chromosomes are intimately intertwined and attached, and various types of mixing of chromosomes can occur when they wrap around each other. This type of general or *homologous recombination* is also known as *crossover*. A single crossover involves the swapping of the parts of two chromosomes at a single point of attachment. Double (triple, etc.) crossover can occur when chromosome parts are swapped at more than one place. When crossover occurs between homologous chromosomes but at two different positions, it is called *unequal crossover*. This results in two chromosomes of unequal length (refer figure 2.1). Some recombinations are non-reciprocal and only one of the offspring is changed by crossover while the other remains unaffected. There are still many other subtle forms of crossover that have not been mentioned here.

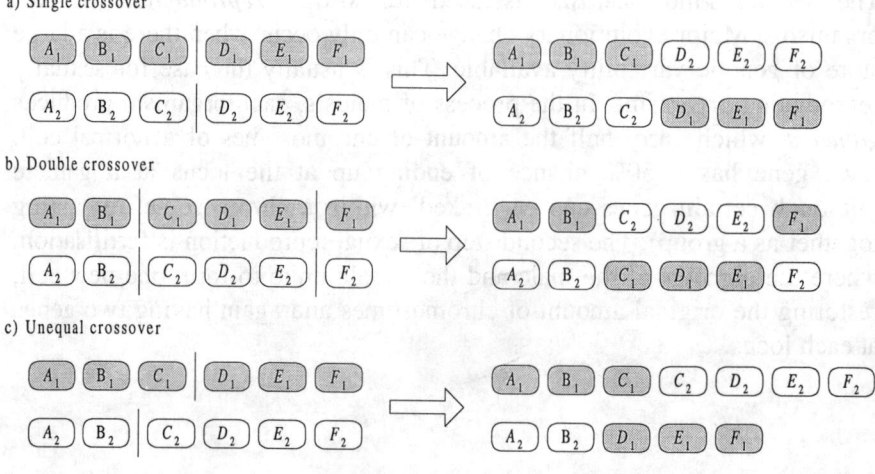

a) Single crossover

b) Double crossover

c) Unequal crossover

Figure 2.1   *Examples of some crossover types*

Gene mutations (also called point mutations) are confined to a change in a single gene only, and are the results of a chemical change in the structure of the gene. They are thought to play the most important part in contributing evolutionary changes to organisms. The effects can be enormous, and although most mutations are deleterious for the organism, the small percentage of mutations that is beneficial provides an increased fitness to the organism and its influence can spread throughout the population over time.

Natural evolution

The most influential theory on evolution was given by Charles Darwin in the last century. His ideas form the basis of most present-day evolutionary theories. Evolution is defined in the field of biology as *a change in the gene pool of a population over time*. It is therefore a population level phenomenon; only groups of organisms evolve. While the kind of evolution described by Darwin normally takes place over very long periods of time and observations are based on fossil records, evolution has actually been directly observed within a span of only several years.

Evolutionary mechanisms can basically be grouped into two categories: those that increase genetic variation and those that decrease it. The mechanisms that increase variation are the mutations occurring during reproduction, as well as a concept called *gene flow*. Gene flow simply means an introduction of new genetic material from another population of the same species by means of migration. The mechanisms decreasing genetic variation are *natural selection* and *genetic drift*. These are now described in further detail.

In Darwinian evolutionary theory, *natural selection* is seen as the creative force of evolution. When supplied with genetic variation it ensures that sexually reproducing species can adapt to changing environments. In the course of evolution, it preserves the favourable part of the variation within a species. It often achieves this by letting the fittest individuals of a species produce the most offspring for the next generation. For instance, in a koala population the male leader, being the fittest individual, has the exclusive right to mate all the females of the population. This provides a *selective pressure* that favours this fitter individual of a population. The theory of natural selection is therefore often referred to as the *survival of the fittest*, however this term is misleading because it is not the survival of the organism in itself that is the driving force of evolution, but rather it is the contribution of this fitter organism's alleles to the next generation's gene pool. Furthermore, the fitness of an organism is not just a measure of its physical abilities, but also a measure of its sexual attractiveness to the other sex. For natural selection to be a creative force, the genetic variation must be random and its effect relatively small, which is the case in present evolutionary theories. Evolution has no direction, nor is there a sense of progress where certain organisms are 'better' than others. Organisms just become better adapted to their environments and the changes made, may in fact prove harmful if the environment alters again.

Even without any selective pressure as contributed by natural selection, there is a mechanism at work that decreases genetic variation. If each animal has an equal chance of producing offspring (i.e. no selective pressure) and there is no mechanism for introducing variation (i.e. no mutation or gene flow), then the variation in alleles would decrease by means of *genetic drift*. Genetic drift is the binomial sampling error of the gene pool. Organisms that reproduce increase the dominance of their alleles over the population. In the next generation the dominance of these alleles is expected to increase even more simply because there is an increased chance that an organism possessing them is chosen to reproduce. Alternatively, if an organism has certain genes, which are unique to the population, but it does not reproduce, then these unique genes would be lost for ever. Due to the constant possibility of decrease in gene variation, a lack of mechanisms to introduce variation would eventually result in a complete lack of genetic variation in the gene pool.

Natural selection does not necessarily have the effect of producing optimal structures or behaviours, in that it may act on the organism as a whole, not on specific traits. Many species are stuck in local optima simply because the transition to a more global optimum is very unlikely. This transition would normally involve having to pass through less viable states and natural selection does not cater for this. The only way the species can reach a state with a higher fitness is by a lucky variation (mutation) or combinations of these. Even being in a very good state does not ensure the species will continue to thrive in the future. A highly specialised and therefore very fit species will have a hard time adapting itself when the environment happens to change. Natural selection has no mechanism that provides future planning; it is purely a local mechanism.

The Darwin machine

The main themes of the evolutionary theory as described previously are commonly referred to as Darwinism. There is strong evidence that evolution is not the only Darwinian process found in nature. On a much smaller time scale of days to weeks a similar process seems to take place when the immune system of an organism produces antibodies to a virus infection. Through a series of cellular generations the immune system evolves antibodies that become better and better ('fitter') in defending the organism against the invaders. This is only one example of an alternative Darwinian process. To abstract from the special Darwinian theories, the concept of a *minimal Darwin machine* is introduced [Calvin, 1994]. A minimal Darwin machine, being a system ruled by a Darwinian process, must have the six essential properties listed in table 2.1. For each property, the corresponding occurrence in Darwinian evolutionary theory is given as an example. The reader can decide whether genetic algorithms, presented in the following paragraphs, fulfil all of these requirements and can thus be regarded as a minimal Darwin machine.

Table 2.1 *The requirements for a minimal Darwin machine, illustrated by their occurrence in Darwinian evolutionary theory*

Requirements	Darwinian evolutionary theory
1. The system operates on patterns of some sort.	*The genotypes are chromosomes, consisting of a string of genes.*
2. Copies are made of these patterns.	*Genotypes are copied by means of (a)sexual reproduction.*
3. During the copying variations occur.	*Genetic mutations occur during reproduction.*
4. The various patterns compete with each other.	*Competition occurs since there is only room and food for a limited amount of organisms in a certain area.*
5. The selective success of a pattern is biased by its environment.	*Natural selection works on the relative fitness of an organism, which depends on the complete state of the system (i.e. the organism and its environment).*
6. Copying only occurs after a certain amount of differential success.	*Only organisms who are fit enough survive until reproductive age and are able to pass on offspring.*

2.2   *The genetic algorithm*

Genetic algorithms were developed by John Holland in the 1970's [Holland, 1975]. They are based on a Darwinian-type survival of the fittest strategy, whereby potential solutions to a problem compete and mate with each other in order to produce increasingly stronger individuals. Each individual in the population represents a potential solution to the problem that is to be solved; i.e. the optimisation of some generally very complex function. These individuals are represented in the genetic algorithm by means of a linear string, similar to the way genetic information in organisms is coded onto chromosomes. In GA terminology the members of a population are therefore referred to as chromosomes. Chromosomes are assembled from a set of genes, that are generally characters belonging to a certain alphabet A. A chromosome can be thought of as a vector x consisting of l genes a_i:

$$x = (a_1, a_2, ..., a_l), \quad a_i \in A_i$$

l is referred to as the length of the chromosome. Commonly all alphabets in a chromosome are the same: $A = A_1 = A_2 = ... = A_l$. The alphabets commonly used today are the cases of binary genes ($A = \{0, 1\}$), and real-valued genes ($A = \mathbb{R}$). In the latter case, the real values can be stored in a gene by means of a fixed or floating point representation or by a conversion to an integer.

In biological systems, a genotype of the total genetic package is a structure made up of several chromosomes. The phenotype is the actual organism formed by the interaction of the genotype with its environment. In genetic algorithms however, an individual is usually represented by a single chromosome, and therefore the chromosome and the genotype are one and the same. The term 'individual' is used for a member of the population where the genotype x of this member refers to the chromosome and the phenotype p to the observed structure acting as a potential solution to the problem. Genetic algorithms therefore rely on a dual representation of individuals where a mapping function is needed between the two representations: the genotype or *representation space* and the phenotype or *problem space*. The fitness of a chromosome is, in general, a mapping of the chromosome x to a real positive value $f(x) \in \mathbb{R}^+$, that measures the individual's performance on the problem. In genetic algorithms this mapping is usually deterministic and constant (independent of time).

Example of an optimisation problem

As an example, consider the problem of optimising the weights for a simple neural network in order for it to perform the exclusive OR task. The neural network in question is a simple one consisting of 2 inputs, 2 hidden neurons and 1 output neuron. All neurons have a connection to the bias unit which has a constant value of 1 (i.e. a standard threshold). The transfer function of the neurons is the sigmoid transfer function.

The aim is to train the network to perform the exclusive-OR (XOR) function, which is described by the input-output mapping of table 2.2. In other words: a set of weights must be found so the neural network performs this XOR function.

Table 2.2   *Training set for the XOR function*

Input vector x	target t(x)
(0,10)	1
(0,−10)	1
(10,0)	0
(−10,0)	0

A chromosome or genotype consists of all the weights of the network, including the bias weights. One gene of a chromosome represents a single weight value. A single genetic algorithm is used with real-valued genes, thus the alphabet is $\mathbb{R}$. The weights of the network are placed on a chromosome as shown in figure 2.2. This figure also demonstrates a clear distinction between the genotype (real-valued numbers on a chromosome) and the phenotype (the values interpreted as the weights of an actual neural network). Such a phenotype is a potential solution to the problem.

Table 2.3   *Initial neuron weights*

$w_{1,0} = 0.0$	$w_{1,1} = 0.25$	$w_{1,2} = 0.25$
$w_{2,0} = -1.0$	$w_{2,1} = 0.0$	$w_{2,2} = 0.2$
$w_{3,0} = -1.6$	$w_{3,1} = 0.0$	$w_{3,2} = 4.0$

a) Genotype: chromosomal representation

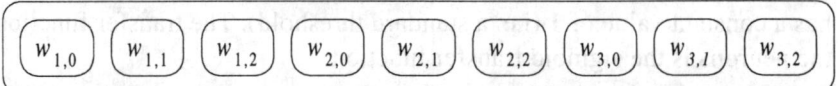

b) Phenotype: resulting neural network

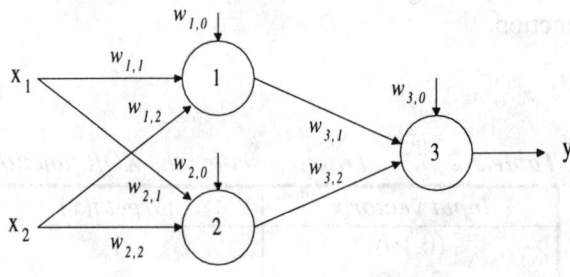

Figure 2.2   *Illustration of a chromosome and its corresponding network*

The fitness function should reflect the individual's performance on the actual problem. For this case, an appropriate fitness function is the inverse of the performance error on the training set of input-output patterns. The inverse of the performance error is used because the standard genetic algorithm searches for the maximum fitness. A low performance error should be reflected in a good performance and therefore a high fitness value.

When the example weights of table 2.3 are used and placed on a chromosome, the following string of genes would result: x = (0.0, 0.25, 0.25, -1.0, 0.0, 0.2, -1.6, 0.0, 4.0). Evaluation of this chromosome places these values into the network and subsequently calculates the performance error, $E(x)$, on the XOR training set using this set of weights:

$$E(x) = \sum_{i=1}^{F} \sum_{j=1}^{N_{out}} \left(O_{i,j}(x) - T_{i,j} \right)^2$$

where: F = the number of training facts in the training set
        N_{out} = the number of outputs of the network
        $O_{i,j}(x)$ = the jth output of the network resulting from training fact i
        $T_{i,j}$ = the jth target output of training fact i

The corresponding fitness, $f(x)$, is then calculated as:

$$f(x) = E_{max} - E(x)$$

The maximum performance error E_{max} would in this case be set equal to 4, as this is the maximum possible value obtainable for $E(x)$. The example chromosome, which classifies 3 out of the four training facts correctly (using a threshold of 0.4), gives a performance error $E(x) = 0.967$, resulting in a fitness of $f(x) = 4 - 0.967 = 3.033$.

Alternatively, the whole procedure of reversing the network error can be performed by a pre-processing stage of the reproduction operator. This will be discussed further in the book. Then, the network errors themselves are without alteration used as raw fitness values.

The algorithm

The following steps describe the operation of a standard genetic algorithm (a more elaborate flow chart of this algorithm is shown in figure 2.3). These steps are described elaborately in the following paragraphs.

1. Randomly create an initial population of chromosomes.
2. Compute the fitness of every member of the current population.
3. If there is a member of the current population that satisfies the problem requirements then stop. Otherwise, continue with the next step.
4. Create an intermediate population by extracting members from the current population using the reproduction or selection operator.
5. Generate a new population by applying the genetic operators crossover and mutation to this intermediate population.
6. Go back to step 2.

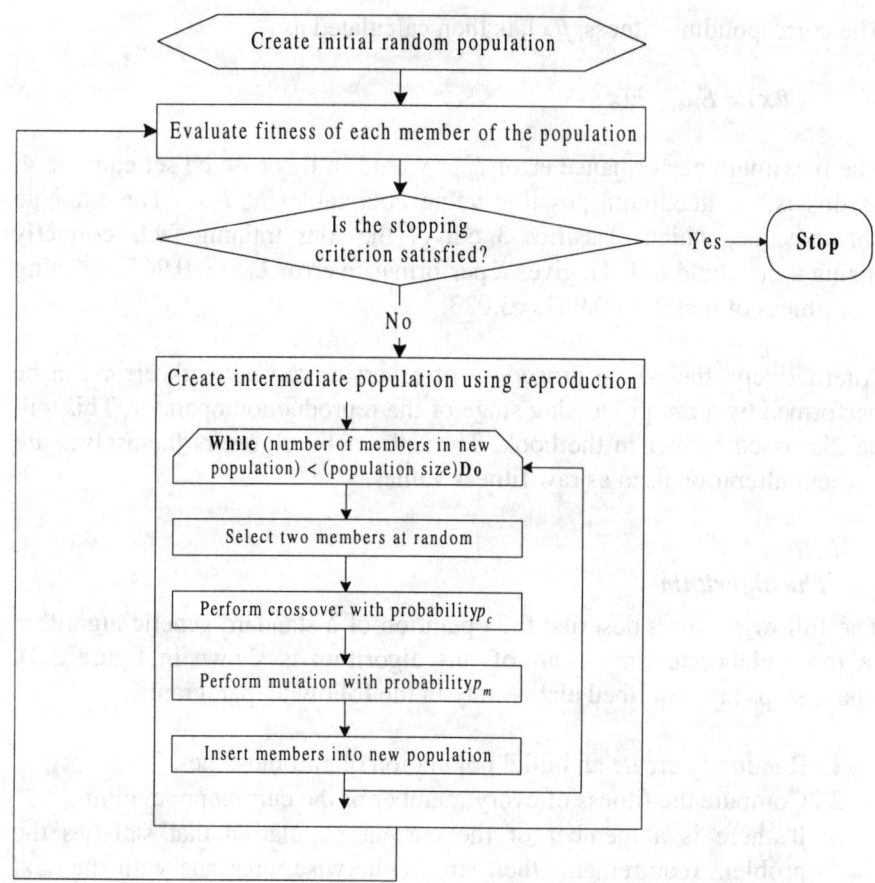

Figure 2.3   *Flow chart of the standard genetic algorithm*

- **Step 1: randomly create an initial population of chromosomes.**
The initial population is filled with chromosomes that have randomly valued genes. For binary valued chromosomes, each gene can take on the values '0' and '1', with equal probability. With real-valued chromosomes, various distributions are possible, for example a uniform or normal distribution in a certain range. The range should be chosen so the resulting values are in a logical scope for the problem at hand.

Another parameter that must be chosen is the size of the population, i.e. how many chromosomes are contained in one generation. There is no fixed optimal value, but in general the following holds: smaller populations (with less than about 50 chromosomes) take less time before they converge to a final solution, larger populations (with more than 50 chromosomes) converge more often to the global optimum. In this context, *convergence* describes the situation where almost all of the chromosomes in a population share the same gene values. Therefore, the following generations will again contain (almost) the same chromosomes, and apart from the effects of mutation, no changes of any consequences will occur in the future. Ideally, the algorithm will converge to the global optimum, however a *premature convergence* to a sub-optimal solution may be observed with small populations. A trade-off must then be found between the two constraints of time to convergence and the probability of actually finding the global optimum.

- **Step 2: Compute the fitness of every member of the current population.**

For every member of the current population, the fitness $f(x)$ is evaluated. An example of this in a neural network was given in the previous section. In most genetic algorithms, this procedure is by far the most time consuming, so care must be taken its implementation.

- **Step 3: If there is a member of the current population that satisfies the problem requirements then stop. Otherwise, continue with the next step.**

The stopping criterion is usually set to the point in time, when an individual has been found that gives an adequate solution to the problem, or alternatively when a set maximum number of generations has been run. It can also be set equal to the point where the population has converged to a single solution, so that no further improvement would be expected from this particular run.

- **Step 4: Create an intermediate population by extracting members from the current population using the reproduction or selection operator.**

There are many possibilities for the extraction of members from the current population. This step can be divided into two stages: *fitness normalisation* and *selection*.

Fitness normalisation is used to force the fitness values of the chromosomes into a certain range, if this is not already taken care of during the fitness calculation itself. Examples of possible normalisations are the addition or subtraction of a certain bias, and inverting ($\frac{a}{f(x)}$) or reversing ($a - f(x)$) the fitness values, in order to minimise rather than maximise the fitness. Another frequently used algorithm is *ranking*, commonly implemented as a kind of pre-processing stage in order to impose a constant selective pressure. The chromosomes are organised in order of their fitness (the chromosome with the lowest fitness receives rank 0, the next worst performer gets rank 1, etc.). After being multiplied by a certain value, these ranking numbers are used by the selection operator instead of the raw fitness values. The multiplication value ensures that the fitnesses of the best and the worst chromosomes in a population always have a fixed ratio, with the others linearly spaced in between. This ranking system ensures that even when the various fitness values are getting close together due to convergence, the best chromosome remains favoured above the worst one to the same extent as in the beginning of the genetic algorithm, improving its terminal convergence. Ranking can also be performed in reverse, giving the fittest chromosome rank 0 and so on. This can be used as an alternative to reversing the fitness values during fitness normalisation, followed by normal ranking.

After these potential pre-processing stages, the reproduction or selection operator selects certain chromosomes and places them into the intermediate population. This is usually completed in consecutive steps, in which two chromosomes are selected, altered by crossover and mutation and inserted into the new population. This operation is demonstrated in the flow chart of figure 2.3. However, since each member of the intermediate population is selected individually, this causes no difference in the procedure of the selection operator.

Commonly, the selection process uses the *roulette wheel* operator. Chromosomes are selected in quantities according to their relative fitness values (after normalisation and/or ranking). The roulette wheel selection method is therefore called a proportionate selection method. The probability that a chromosome x is selected, is equal to its relative fitness. Thus:

$$P_{select}(x) = \frac{f(x)}{\sum f}$$

The roulette wheel operator is best visualised by imagining a wheel where each chromosome occupies an area that is related to its fitness. An example of such a roulette wheel can be seen in figure 2.4, which is based on the chromosome information of table 2.4.

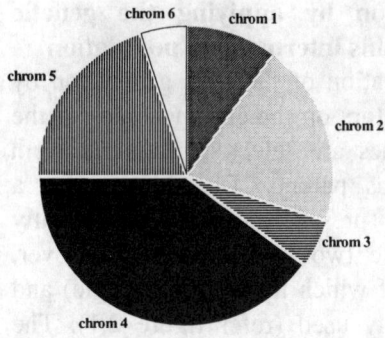

Table 2.4   *Chromosome information*

Chrom.	$f(x)$	$p_{select}(x)$	$E_{select}(x)$
1	2	0.10	0.6
2	4	0.20	1.2
3	1	0.05	0.3
4	8	0.40	2.4
5	4	0.20	1.2
6	1	0.05	0.3
	$\Sigma f = 20$	$\Sigma p = 1$	$\Sigma E = 6$

Figure 2.4   *Roulette wheel*

Selecting a chromosome can be thought of as spinning the roulette wheel. When the wheel stops, a fixed marker determines which chromosome will be selected. This is repeated until the number of chromosomes required for the intermediate population is obtained. Since the expected number of times that chromosome x will be selected is given by $E_{select}(x) = N \cdot p_{select}(x)$, where N is the population size, this can be expressed as:

$$E_{select}(x) = \frac{f(x)}{\bar{f}}$$

where $\bar{f}$ is the average fitness of the population.

Other possible selection operators, apart from the roulette wheel, include the *uniform* selection operator, where each chromosome has an equal chance of selection regardless of its fitness, and the *tournament* selection operator. With this last method, a typically small number of chromosomes (for example 4) is uniformly chosen, after which they compete with each other on the basis of their fitness values. Only the fittest chromosome is actually passed on to the intermediate population. Another operator, *integral* selection, is based on the calculated values for E_{select} for each chromosome, similar to the roulette wheel operator. However, it differs by guaranteeing that each chromosome x is selected at least as many times as its corresponding value of $E_{select}(x)$ predicts (rounded towards zero), in order to reduce the role of chance.

- **Step 5: Generate a new population by applying the genetic operators crossover and mutation to this intermediate population.**

The next step involves forming the population of the next generation by applying the crossover and mutation operators on the chromosomes of the intermediate population. Two chromosomes are selected randomly from this intermediate population and serve as parents. Depending upon a probabilistic chance p_c, the crossover rate (preset by the user and usually close to 1.0), it is decided whether these two will undergo crossover. Various types of crossover are possible, of which the *1-point* (single) and *2-point* (double) types are most frequently used (refer figure 2.1). The crossover points are chosen randomly from the available potential crossover sites. In general, *n-point (n < l)* crossover can be used, or alternatively, *uniform* crossover where each site between any two neighbouring genes is a potential crossover point. Each of these potential crossover points has a probability of 0.5 that it will be used as a crossover point. For real-valued gene types, there are more possible crossover types that exist, such as a *linear interpolation* between the two values in the same gene position, in combination with for instance 2-point crossover. Examples of uniform and linear interpolation crossover are given in figure 2.5.

After the potential application of the crossover operator, each of the genes of the resulting chromosomes is subject to possible mutation. Similarly, this depends on a probabilistic chance p_m, the mutation rate, which is usually a value close to zero. For binary genes, mutation inverts a bit value, or re-initialises it with a random value. Again, more sophisticated options are available for real-valued genes: inverting, re-initialisation with a certain distribution or addition of a value with a certain probabilistic distribution.

a) Uniform crossover

b) Linear interpolation 2-point crossover

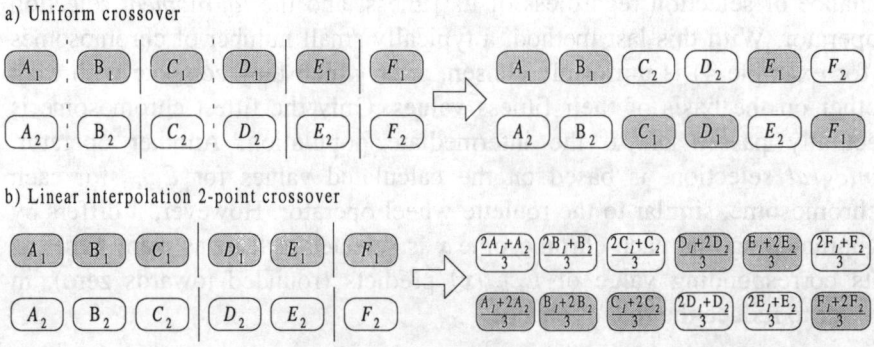

Figure 2.5   *Examples of the 'uniform' and 'linear interpolation 2-point' crossover types*

After these genetic operators, the resulting chromosomes are inserted into the new population (the next generation). If neither the crossover nor the mutation operator has been applied to the two chromosomes, the resulting chromosomes will be identical to those in the previous generation. This step is repeated until the new population reaches the set population size. If the population size is not an even number, it will be necessary to randomly select one of the last pair of chromosomes created to complete the generation. Random selection is also necessary when the population size is even and the *elitism* scheme is used. In elitism, the fittest chromosome of the current population is transferred to the next generation unaltered. This scheme has the advantage that once a very fit individual has been found, it cannot be lost again due to an unfortunate crossover or mutation. Experience has shown that it is almost always very advantageous to use elitism.

Solving the example problem

As an example, the previously introduced exclusive OR problem will be solved using a genetic algorithm.

- **Initialisation and evaluation.**

The population size is set to 10. The weights will be initialised using a Gaussian distribution around 0, with an standard deviation of 5, ensuring that most of the weights will be in the range of −10 to +10. The network error of the phenotype on the test data will be used as the raw fitness value (reverse ranking will be applied before selection). This gives the chromosomes of the initial population (generation 0), as shown in table 2.5. Chromosome no. 1 has the smallest network error, and therefore receives the highest value for p_{select}, which is indeed 5 times higher than the selection probability of chromosome no. 5, that shows the worst performance.

Table 2.5   *Details of the initial population (values are rounded)*

No.	Chromosome contents (gene values)									Network Error	$p_{select}(x)$
0	-0.95	-0.33	-6.00	-3.06	-6.95	0.84	1.13	0.50	-2.10	1.26	0.152
1	-8.51	1.64	-3.23	-2.75	0.39	1.98	-2.10	5.41	3.80	1.03	0.167
2	-1.86	-7.14	11.0	-5.13	5.16	8.37	8.71	1.95	-1.13	2.00	0.063
3	-4.66	1.77	-3.92	-5.73	-16.1	-9.65	3.98	-1.97	3.08	1.78	0.122
4	-1.51	-6.28	-4.34	2.52	10.6	2.79	-3.46	4.30	-11.3	1.58	0.137
5	-3.88	6.08	-9.23	-7.68	3.61	2.23	-2.41	-5.03	-6.21	2.01	0.033
6	-7.29	-2.57	-3.05	-0.59	1.82	-0.02	-5.65	-8.61	-2.78	2.00	0.078
7	-2.78	-3.40	-3.91	2.17	1.44	1.27	2.19	9.59	-11.8	2.00	0.048
8	-5.53	-14.5	-7.41	2.91	1.73	-3.31	4.05	1.57	2.92	1.99	0.093
9	14.6	6.60	2.94	-4.04	-3.52	-3.64	-5.85	-5.33	0.96	1.99	0.107

- **Selection, crossover and mutation.**

A reverse linear ranking mechanism will be used to maintain constant selective pressure. The ratio *best* : *worst* is chosen to be 5, resulting in the values for p_{select} as shown in table 2.5. The roulette wheel operator is used to select the intermediate population, with elitism. Standard 2-point crossover is used, with a crossover rate of $p_c = 0.8$. For the mutation operator, Gaussian addition is used (SD = 1.0), applied with a mutation rate of $p_m = 0.1$.

After one generation, the population consists of the chromosomes shown in table 2.6. It indicates chromosome no. 1, which performed best in the initial population, has remained unaltered due to the elitism scheme. It appears that it is still the best performing chromosome, together with chromosome no. 0, which is now identical. The chromosome contents in table 2.6 clearly show that many chromosomes already share one or more gene values, as would be expected due to the fairly high selective pressure and relatively low mutation rate. The average network error of the whole population has dropped from 1.7631 in the initial generation to 1.4846.

Table 2.6 *Details of the population after one generation (values are rounded)*

No.	Chromosome contents (gene values)									Network Error	$p_{select}(x)$
0	-8.51	1.64	-3.23	-2.75	0.39	1.98	-2.10	5.41	3.80	1.03	0.152
1	-8.51	1.64	-3.23	-2.75	0.39	1.98	-2.10	5.41	3.80	1.03	0.167
2	-0.94	-0.33	-6.00	-3.06	-6.95	0.84	1.13	0.50	-2.10	1.26	0.122
3	14.6	6.60	2.94	-5.73	-16.1	-9.65	3.98	-1.97	3.08	1.79	0.078
4	-4.66	1.77	-3.92	-4.04	-3.52	-3.64	-5.85	-4.55	0.96	1.99	0.048
5	-0.95	-2.57	-3.05	-3.65	-6.95	0.84	1.13	0.50	-2.10	1.27	0.107
6	-0.95	-0.33	-6.00	-3.06	-6.95	0.84	-0.03	0.50	-2.10	1.21	0.137
7	-7.29	-0.33	-6.00	-0.59	1.82	-0.02	-5.65	-8.61	-3.19	2.00	0.033
8	-4.66	-0.33	-6.00	-3.06	-16.1	-9.65	3.98	-1.97	3.08	1.96	0.063
9	-0.95	1.77	-3.92	-5.73	-7.08	0.84	1.13	0.50	-2.10	1.29	0.093

Figure 2.6 indicates the network error of the fittest chromosome of each generation (minimum), as well as the average network error (mean) of the whole population. After 18 generations, an individual is found that successfully classifies all four test samples and after a total of 25 generations the genetic algorithm is stopped. In the last 7 generations, the network error was still reduced significantly. It also appears that after 18 generations, for each gene, an average of 7 of the 10 chromosomes share

the same allele. This demonstrates that the diversity of the various genes can decrease rapidly after only a few generations. The graph also demonstrates elitism: the minimum network error never increases between generations, unlike the mean network error which can increase temporarily and regularly does so.

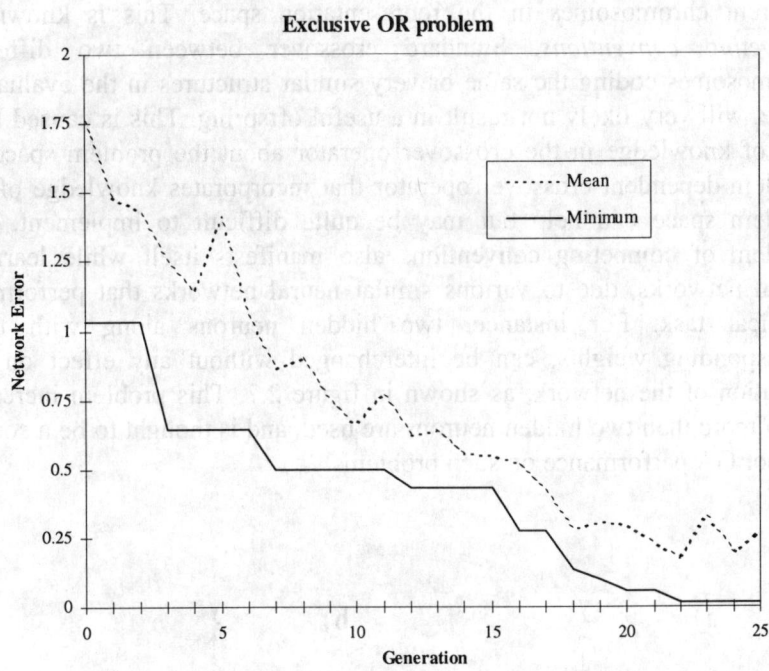

Figure 2.6   *Results of the genetic algorithm (minimum and mean of population)*

A few remarks on genetic algorithms

Competing conventions, epistasis, steady state genetic algorithms and parallel genetic algorithms further consider genetic algorithms function in general, and also the operation of these algorithms in the field of neural network weight optimisation.

• **Competing conventions**

Genetic algorithms depend upon two separate representational spaces. One is the *representation space* or *genotype space*, where the genetic operators (crossover and mutation) are performed on the strings or genotypes. The other space is the *evaluation space* or *phenotype space*, where the problem structures of phenotypes are evaluated on their ability to perform the task and their fitness is calculated. The evaluation space is frequently called *problem space*. The genetic operators usually perform their task on the genotypes without any knowledge of their interpretation in the evaluation space. This works well providing the interpretation function is such that the application of the genetic operators in the representation space leads to appropriate points in the evolution space. Problems occur when a structure in the evaluation space (e.g. a neural network) can be represented by very different chromosomes in the representation space. This is known as *competing conventions*. Standard crossover between two different chromosomes coding the same or very similar structures in the evaluation space, will very likely not result in a useful offspring. This is caused by a lack of knowledge in the crossover operator about the problem space. A problem dependent crossover operator that incorporates knowledge of the problem space can help but may be quite difficult to implement. The problem of competing conventions also manifests itself while learning neural networks, due to various similar neural networks that perform an identical task. For instance, two hidden neurons along with their corresponding weights, can be interchanged without any effect on the operation of the network, as shown in figure 2.7. This problem increases when more than two hidden neurons are used, and is thought to be a source of poor GA performance on such problems.

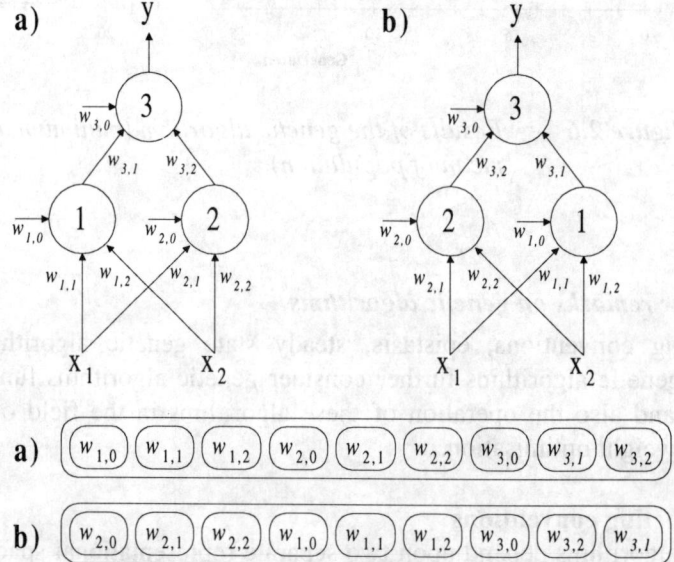

Figure 2.7   *Illustration of competing conventions: network a and b have equal functionality, but completely different genotypes.*

- **Epistasis**

Similar to biology, epistasis can be observed in genetic algorithms. Taking the neural network as an example, it is clear that well trained hidden neurons have no effect unless the output neurons make good use of them. This can be observed as a form of epistasis, where some genes (representing weights in the network) are able to render others useless. Problems with a high degree of epistasis are often difficult for a genetic algorithm to solve.

- **Steady State Genetic Algorithm**

Instead of allowing the algorithm to make successive generations, it is possible to create a limited number of new chromosomes at one time, and insert those back into the old population to take the place of other chromosomes which are discarded. These 'doomed' chromosomes can be selected with various methods: *uniform replacement*, selecting the doomed chromosomes randomly, *ranked replacement*, selecting the chromosomes with the lowest fitness, or *parental replacement*, selecting the parents of the newly generated chromosomes for replacement. Of course, many more exotic replacement schemes can be used. The insertion can be made optional by letting the new chromosomes replace the old ones only if they possess a higher fitness (otherwise the newly generated chromosomes are discarded again). This approach is called a Steady State Genetic Algorithm (SSGA). More commonly it is known as a 'Genitor'-type algorithm, due to the fact that 'Genitor', a widely used GA-package developed by J. Grefenstette, is based on SSGA. A slight advantage is that SSGA requires somewhat less memory as only one population instead of two needs to be stored. A disadvantage however is the fact that, due to the extreme selective pressure of SSGAs, the initial population tends to lose its diversity within a few generations, potentially discarding valuable genetic information.

When an SSGA is used with a small population and the selection and replacement mechanisms are ranked, it is observed that the population loses its diversity within only a few generations. In other words: they are usually in a continuous state of premature convergence. SSGAs begin performing a so-called stochastic hill-climbing search, continuously trying out new solutions very similar to the old ones, as only the mutation operator can introduce new alleles. With an increase in fitness, the whole population 'moves' in that direction, as the newly found highly fit alleles spread over the remainder of the population.

- **Parallel genetic algorithms**

Genetic algorithms can be very successfully implemented as a parallel system. As stated before, the evaluation of the chromosomes is by far the most time consuming part of the algorithm. This part can be very naturally implemented in parallel across the population, resulting in a substantial increase of speed of the total algorithm. A second possible parallelisation is possible if multiple (sub)populations are used, each performing their own search and occasionally interacting with each other.

• Overview

The differences between genetic algorithms and Darwinian evolutionary theory lie mainly in terms of scale. In biology, very large populations take millions of years to evolve properly. In contrast, genetic algorithms use very small populations and are supposed to develop solutions after only a few generations. This is the main reason for the relatively high mutation rate used in genetic algorithms, necessary in order to compensate for the lack of high diversity in genes which is caused by the premature convergence of these small populations. Another important difference between the two, genetic algorithms can be regarded to 'live to improve' in order to solve a problem, whereas biological evolutionary systems merely 'improve to live', without any higher goal.

The SUGAL genetic algorithms package

The genetic algorithms package used in the research for this book is SUGAL v2.0. SUGAL is the SUnderland Genetic ALgorithm package, developed by Dr. A. Hunter at the University of Sunderland, England[1]. It is a package, written in 'C' and available for both Unix and Windows platforms, designed for experimentation with genetic algorithms and related techniques. It is intended to be used in GA research. Consequently, the major emphasis is on providing a large number of options, configurability and extensibility. Efficiency is considered important, but has been sacrificed where it would conflict with the above requirements.

A major feature of SUGAL is that the user must program a method of evaluating encoded solutions to a problem. The package itself is not dedicated to any problem, it simply handles chromosomes without consideration of how they are used. The user must perform the interpretation and translation of the chromosomes into phenotypes and evaluate their fitness. The remainder is handled by the GA engine of the SUGAL package. For neural network learning, this means that code must be written to translate a chromosome into a neural network, to present the test samples to this network and calculate its network error. This network error is then passed back to SUGAL as the fitness measure of the particular chromosome.

---

[1] Available via the World Wide Web at http://osiris.sund.ac.uk/ahu/sugal/home.html

As it stands, the package is highly suitable for user extension, such as a new crossover operator without need for intervention in the existing source code. However, it proved to be very useful for neural network optimisation to make some alterations to the core of the package. These modifications included general options, such as more elaborate file output routines, and also neural network specific changes, such as displaying the percentage of test patterns which were correctly classified by the fittest member of the current population, and being able to stop the algorithm after a 100% score has been achieved. Furthermore, many efficiency optimisations have been performed in order to make the process of running a genetic algorithm faster. This has resulted in an approximately 200% increase in speed, not unimportant for this kind of time-consuming simulations.

An important option in SUGAL is the possibility of performing multiple runs automatically, each time with different parameters, while calculating various statistics of the algorithm's performance. This enables the user to alter the crossover rate in small steps and perform several independent runs for each setting, while automatically collecting the required statistics, such as the mean fitness of the best chromosome of the population for the various runs with the same crossover rate. This feature of SUGAL has also been elaborately altered and extended, in order to make it more user friendly and offer more possibilities.

3. Mathematical Foundations of Genetic Algorithms

Genetic algorithms can be described as 'living things' in that they cannot easily be captured in mathematical equations to predict their behaviour. In fact, similar to neural networks, the genetic algorithms involve many variants with various characteristics. To date, there is no foundational theory in sight which can fully capture the working of the genetic algorithms.

Nevertheless, steps have been taken to formulate the mathematical foundation of genetic algorithms. To explain the operation of genetic algorithms, and certainly to give useful insights into what makes these genetic algorithms work, several approaches have resulted in a number of theories, such as the *Schema Theorem*, the *Building Block Hypothesis*, the *Walsh-Schema Transform* and the application of *Markov Chain Analysis*. The first two theories form a mathematical background for the remainder of this book, and will be presented in this chapter in some depth. A brief explanation and summary of the latter two will be given, since they do not enter into the genetic algorithms specific to this book and are only included for completeness.

3.1 The Schema Theorem

The Schema Theorem, introduced by Holland, is widely accepted as an important milestone in genetic algorithms [Holland, 1975]. Since its presentation, several researchers have developed additions to Holland's basic form, accounting for variation in the length of the chromosomes and for real-coded chromosomes [Antonisse, 1989]. For simplicity, Holland's concepts will be presented here in their basic form.

First some related terms are defined. The *search space* Ω is the complete set of possible chromosomes or strings as they are referred to by Holland. In case of chromosomes of a fixed length l where each gene can take on a value in the alphabet A of size k, the resulting size of the search space is k^l. For example, in the case of a binary chromosome (alphabet size $k = 2$) with 8 genes (chromosome length $l = 8$), the size of the search space would be $2^8 = 256$, resulting in 256 possible different chromosomes. A string in the population S is denoted by a vector $x \in \Omega$. So, in the previously described example, x would be an element of $\{0,1\}^8$. The number of instances of a string x in the total population S is denoted by $m(x)$.

Schemata

A *schema* is a similarity template that defines a subset of strings with fixed equal genes at certain positions. A schema therefore defines a subset of the complete search space, or a *hyperplane partition* of this search space. Similar to the hyperplanes of neural networks, these hyperplane partitions are formed by the gene values of a chromosome (similar to the weight values in the case of the neural networks). In the case of the neural network hyperplanes, the weight values are all fixed and define a single hyperplane (an area) in the input space of possible input vectors x. In the case of the schemata, hyperplane partitions are formed in the search space Ω, defined by all possible gene combinations, or in other words: in the gene (or weight) space itself. Hyperplane partitions are sub-volumes of this gene space, restricted by the fixed values of the schema. Every extra fixed value, for a particular position of the schema, limits the resulting space of chromosomes that can still be formed.

A schema H is a string of the same length as the length of the chromosomes. Each position in this string can take on the values of the alphabet of the chromosomes, in which case this position is called *fixed*, plus a "don't care" character '*'. So in the binary case, schemata are defined as $H \in \{0, 1, *\}^l$. Using the previous example of an 8-bit binary chromosome, a possible schema could be:

$$H_1 = \{\, 0 * 1\, 0\, 1 * 1\, 0 \,\}$$

This particular schema would describe the following subset of the search space:

$$\{ (0\,0\,1\,0\,1\,0\,1\,0),$$
$$(0\,0\,1\,0\,1\,1\,1\,0),$$
$$(0\,1\,1\,0\,1\,0\,1\,0),$$
$$(0\,1\,1\,0\,1\,1\,1\,0) \}$$

The term *order* is also used in relation to the schema, where it defines the number of fixed positions in this schema. In the above example, this would lead to an order of the schema, denoted by $O(H_1)$, of six. The search space Ω itself can be defined by a schema of order zero, with a "don't care" symbol at every position. In this case: $\Omega = \{\, * * * * * * * * \,\}$. The number of schemata possible is $(k + 1)^l$; in the example, $(2 + 1)^8 = 6561$ possible schemata.

The *defining length* of a schema, denoted by $\delta(H)$, is the distance between the first and the last fixed positions of a schema, ranging from zero in schemata with 0 or 1 fixed positions, up to l-1 in schemata with all positions fixed.

Finally, the number of strings in the population belonging to schema H, denoted by $m(H)$, is given by $m(H) = \sum_{x \in H} m(x)$. Note that x has to be a member of the population.

In the schema theorem, let the population at time t be defined by $S(t)$, and let $m(H,t)$ denote the number of strings in this population belonging to a certain schema H. The average fitness of all the strings in the present population representing schema H is defined as:

$$f(H,t) = \frac{\sum_{x \in H} f(x) \cdot m(x)}{m(H,t)} \tag{3.1}$$

$f(H,t)$ is also called the *average pay-off function* of schema H. If the fitness of a string x is equal to $f(x)$, the standard roulette wheel selection mechanism would result in an expected number of selections of x given by $E(x) = f(x)/\bar{f}(t)$, where $\bar{f}(t)$ stands for the average fitness of all the strings in the population at time t. This leads to the following expression of the expected number of strings belonging to schema H in the next population[1]:

$$m(H,t+1) = m(H,t) \cdot \frac{f(H,t)}{\bar{f}(t)} \tag{3.2}$$

This equation indicates that schemata with above average fitness values (where $f(H,t) > \bar{f}(t)$), will reproduce in increasing numbers in successive generations, while schemata with below average fitness values ($f(H,t) < \bar{f}(t)$) will do the opposite and eventually die off. When $a = f(H,t)/\bar{f}(t)$ is relatively constant, equation (3.2) can be approximated by a linear difference equation of the form $m(H,t+1) = a \cdot m(H,t)$. The solution is given by:

---

[1] It is important to note that at this stage no genetic operator (crossover or mutation) is applied to the selected strings before they are inserted into the next population. The following sections will present additions to the given equations, accounting for the effects caused by these operators.

$$m(H,t) = m(H,0) \cdot a^t \qquad\qquad (3.3)$$

Exponential growth is expected for the strings in the population belonging to above average schemata, while strings belonging to below average schemata are expected to decline exponentially. However, the imposed condition of a constant a would not hold for many generations, as an increase of above average strings and a decrease of below average strings would automatically result in an increase of the average fitness value $\bar{f}(t)$, while $f(H,t)$ would most likely remain relatively constant. This upsets the imposed condition of a constant a. This is also seen when considering that, with a certain fixed population size s, the number of strings in the population belonging to a certain schema H can never exceed s. A situation which is more likely to occur is therefore an initially exponential increase of above average schemata, followed by a slower increase and eventually an almost constant number of strings belonging to schema H, when a has decreased towards a value near 1. In this final stage, the above average schema H has spread over the whole population, so that every member of the population belongs to this schema. This makes $f(H,t)$ by definition equal to $\bar{f}(t)$ and so makes a equal to 1. Figure 3.1 gives a visual example of the spread of an above average schema H over the population. For each generation, the average pay-off function $f(H,t)$ and the average fitness $\bar{f}(t)$ are given, as well as the growth coefficient a. From this a, the expected number of chromosomes in the next generation, belonging to schema H, can be calculated by the linear difference equation.

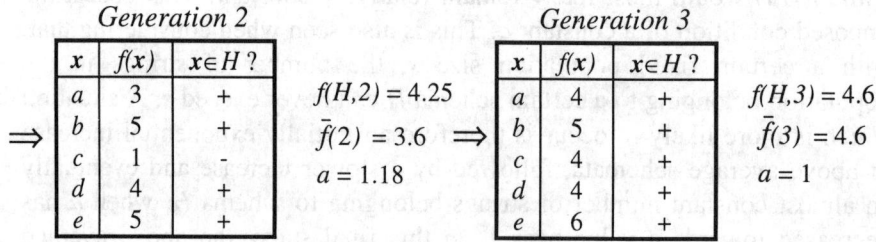

Generation 0

x	f(x)	x∈H ?
a	1	-
b	2	-
c	0	-
d	1	-
e	4	+

$f(H,0) = 4$
$\bar{f}(0) = 1.6 \Rightarrow$
$a = 2.5$

Generation 1

x	f(x)	x∈H ?
a	1	-
b	5	+
c	1	-
d	1	-
e	4	+

$f(H,1) = 4.5$
$\bar{f}(1) = 2.4 \Rightarrow$
$a = 1.9$

Generation 2

$\Rightarrow$

x	f(x)	x∈H ?
a	3	+
b	5	+
c	1	-
d	4	+
e	5	+

$f(H,2) = 4.25$
$\bar{f}(2) = 3.6 \Rightarrow$
$a = 1.18$

Generation 3

x	f(x)	x∈H ?
a	4	+
b	5	+
c	4	+
d	4	+
e	6	+

$f(H,3) = 4.6$
$\bar{f}(3) = 4.6$
$a = 1$

Figure 3.1   *Example of the spread over the population of an above average schema H*

The effect of crossover

In this section, the effect of the crossover operator on schemata is investigated. When a string belonging to a schema H, recombines with another string into two offspring, the schema will or will not survive crossover. In this light, crossover is a disruptive operator. The survival probability of a schema depends upon its defining length and the type of crossover which has been applied, and is most effectively illustrated with an example. Consider a string x that is selected for 1-point crossover, and two second order schemata H_1 and H_2 of which our string x is an element:

$$
\begin{aligned}
x &= (\ 0 \quad 1 \quad 0 \quad 0 \qquad 1 \quad 1 \quad 0 \quad 1\ ) \\
H_1 &= \{\ * \quad 1 \quad 0 \quad * \qquad * \quad * \quad * \quad * \ \} \\
H_2 &= \{\ * \quad 1 \quad * \quad * \qquad * \quad * \quad 0 \quad * \ \} \\
&\qquad\qquad\qquad\quad \uparrow
\end{aligned}
$$

The crossover point shown above is randomly chosen to be between positions 4 and 5. Unless the other parent string with which x mates also belongs to schema H_2, a possibility that will be ignored for now, schema H_2 will not survive. Schema H_1 however does survive the crossover operator, and (at least) one of the two offspring will also belong to schema H_1. It is clear that schema H_1 has a greater chance of surviving this crossover operator than schema H_2, which has a greater chance of being destroyed due to its longer defining length. Only a crossover between positions 2 and 3 will destroy schema H_1, where schema H_2 will be destroyed by every crossover except those between positions 1 and 2 or between positions 7 and 8. The defining lengths for the schemata are: $\delta(H_1) = 3 - 2 = 1$ and $\delta(H_2) = 7 - 2 = 5$. Generally speaking, a schema of order k survives 1-point crossover if the crossover-site falls outside its defining length. This analysis has led to considerable discussion of the 'representational bias' built into 1-point crossover, namely that this type of crossover is a great deal more disruptive to schemata with long defining lengths than to schemata with short defining lengths. Assuming that the crossover site is chosen randomly from the $l-1$ possible locations, the probability for disruption, denoted by p_d, of a schema of order k, denoted by H_k, is:

$$p_d(H_k) \leq \frac{\delta(H_k)}{l-1} \tag{3.4}$$

This result is upper bound because of the possibility that the other parental string also (partly) belongs to schema H, in which case it may not be destroyed by crossover. The probability of this situation must be deducted from the disruption probability, hence the upper bound.

De Jong extended this analysis to n-point crossover [De Jong, 1975], by noting that no disruption can occur if there are an even number of crossover points (including 0) between each of the defining positions of a schema. Hence, the bound for the disruption of n-point crossover is:

$$p_d(n, H_k) \leq 1 - p_{k,even}(n, H_k) \tag{3.5}$$

where $P_{k,even}(n, H_k)$ is defined to be the probability that an even number of the n crossover points will fall between each of the k defining positions of schema H_k. De Jong provided an exact expression for $P_{k,even}$ for the special case of second order schemata (i.e., $k = 2$):

$$p_{2,even}(n, l, \delta) = \sum_{i=0}^{\left\lfloor \frac{n}{2} \right\rfloor} \binom{n}{2i} \left(\frac{\delta}{l}\right)^{2i} \left(\frac{l-\delta}{l}\right)^{n-2i} \tag{3.6}$$

where $\delta = \delta(H_2)$ and l is the length of schema H_2. The above expression is the probability that an even number of crossover points will fall within the 2nd order schema defined by l and $\delta(H_2)$. The second term of the summation is the probability of placing an even number of crossover points within the 2 defining points. The third term is the probability of placing the remaining crossover points outside the two defining points. Finally, the combinatorial term $\binom{n}{2i}$ represents the number of ways an even number of points can be drawn from the n crossover points. The family of curves generated by this equation (refer figure 3.2) provides considerable insight into the change in disruptive effects on second order schemata as the number of crossover points is increased. It primarily follows that for crossover types with an odd number of points, the operators become increasingly disruptive as the defining length increases. For crossover types with an even number of points, the operators are most disruptive when the defining length is in the range of half the length of the schemata, and gradually become less disruptive as they move away from this value. Since $P_{k.even}$ guarantees no disruption, the main goal is to increase it whenever possible. By taking an even number of crossover points, the representational bias of crossover can be reduced, although it comes at the cost of a slight increase in disruption for the shorter definition length schemata.

Spears and De Jong extended this analysis of crossover disruption even further [Spears and De Jong, 1991], resulting in a recursive relation for $P_{k.even}(n,H_k)$. They also attempted to give further bounds for $p_d(n,H_k)$ by making several assumptions on the probability of both parents sharing the same alleles, so that an odd number of crossover points between defining positions does not always result in disruptive behaviour. This concept however, falls outside the scope of this book.

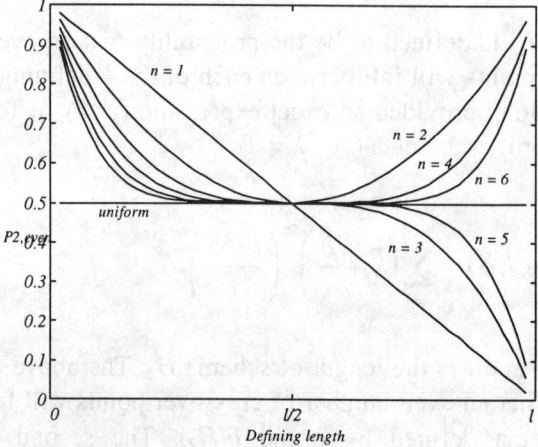

Figure 3.2   *n-point crossover disruption on 2nd order schemata*

Finally, the case of uniform crossover is considered. It is possible to give a more simple expression for the probability of disruption of the schemata of various defining lengths:

$$P_d(H_k) \leq 1 - p_{k,even}(H_k) \tag{3.7}$$

where

$$P_{k,even}(H_k) = \left(\tfrac{1}{2}\right)^{k-1}$$

This can be understood by thinking of uniform crossover as a mask of length l of 0's and 1's, indicating which parent's allele will be utilised at each position (note that this definition is independent of the alphabet size used by the alleles). Scanning the mask from left to right, a switch from 0 to 1 or from 1 to 0 represents a crossover point. Since at every position a 0 or a 1 is equally likely to occur, each possible mask has an equal probability of being generated. Noting that an even number of crossover points between the defining positions of schema H_k corresponds to masks which have either all 0's or all 1's on these defining positions, leads to above equations. In conclusion, uniform crossover removes any representational bias, due to its complete independence from the defining length of a schema. However, the cost for this lack of representational bias is a higher disruption overall (refer figure 3.2), especially for higher order schemata ($O(H_k) = k \geq 3$).

Regardless of the type of crossover used, it is applied with a probability p_c (the crossover rate). Therefore, the probability of disruption by a crossover operator must be multiplied by this value, which gives the general disruption probability for crossover:

$$P_{d,crossover} = p_c \cdot p_d(H_k) \tag{3.8}$$

The effect of mutation

The standard mutation operator can destroy a schema if it is applied to any of its defining positions. The probability that mutation is performed is equal to p_m. Therefore, the chance that a schema of order k is destroyed by this operator, which is equal to 1 minus the chance that every defining position has survived, is given by:

$$P_{d,mutation} = 1 - (1 - p_m)^k \approx p_m \cdot k \qquad \text{for} \quad p_m \ll 1 \tag{3.9}$$

The effects combined: the Schema Theorem

To see the effect of both genetic operators combined, the equations (3.8) and (3.9) are rewritten in the form of survival probabilities p_s, as opposed to disruption:

$$p_{s,crossover} = 1 - p_c \cdot p_d(H_k)$$
$$p_{s,mutation} = 1 - p_m \cdot k$$

The probabilities can then be multiplied since they are applied independently. Neglecting the small cross-product term, the combination with expression (2) gives the Schema Theorem:

$$m(H_k, t+1) \geq m(H_k, t) \cdot \frac{f(H_k, t)}{\bar{f}(t)} \cdot (1 - p_m \cdot k - p_c \cdot p_d(H_k)) \qquad (3.10)$$

The Schema Theorem is only directly applicable to a single generation cycle, however does provide an intuitive feel for the dynamics of genetic algorithms. The usual interpretation of equation (3.10) is often described as: *"The Schema Theorem predicts that schemata with higher than average payoff will be allocated more trials over time, while those with below average payoff will be allocated fewer trials."* Strictly speaking, the word *observed* should be inserted before both occurrences of *payoff*, since the fitness of the schemata is calculated using the present population. The fitness of these strings aim to give a good representation of the general average fitness of these schemata, but it is not guaranteed.

How many schemata are processed usefully?

Finally, it can be shown that the number of schemata which are efficiently processed in each generation is of the order N^3, with N the population size. This property of genetic algorithms helps explain their performance on many optimisation problems and is known as *implicit parallelism* [Goldberg, 1989].

Consider a population of N binary strings of length l. Only schemata that survive with a probability greater than a constant p_s are considered. As a result, assuming the operation of 1-point crossover and a small mutation rate, only those schemata with an error rate $\varepsilon < 1 - p_s$ are admitted, resulting in only schemata with length $l_s < \varepsilon(l-1) + 1$. With a particular schema length, a lower bound on the number of unique schemata, processed by an initially random population of strings, can be calculated. To do this, first the number of schemata of length l_s or less is counted. This is then multiplied by an appropriate population size, chosen such that, on average, no more than one of each schema of length $l_s/2$ is expected.

The number of schemata can be calculated by sliding a template of length l_s over the string with length l. In this template, the last cell is fixed to prevent schemata from being counted multiple times, and the first l_s-1 cells can either take on the fixed value or a "don't care". Clearly, there are $2^{(l_s-1)}$ of these schemata. The total number of these schemata is counted by sliding the template one space at the time over the whole string. This can be done $l - l_s + 1$ times, estimating the total amount of schemata of length l_s or less as $(l - l_s + 1) \cdot 2^{(l_s-1)}$ in this particular string. If this number of schemata is multiplied by N, the correct count of the number of schemata in the whole population would be overestimated, since there will be duplicates of low-order schemata in large populations. Instead, a population size of $N = 2^{l_s/2}$ is chosen, so that one or fewer of all schemata of order $l_s/2$ or more is expected. Recognising that the number of schemata is binomially distributed, so that half are of higher order than $l_s/2$ and half are of lower order, a lower bound on the number of schemata n_s can be estimated by counting only the higher order ones:

$$n_s \geq N \cdot (l - l_s + 1) \cdot 2^{l_s-2} \tag{3.11}$$

The restriction of the population size to the particular value of $N = 2^{l_s/2}$ results in the expression:

$$n_s = \frac{(l - l_s + 1)}{4} N^3 = c \cdot N^3 \tag{3.12}$$

This means that the number of schemata n_s, processed by the population, is of order N^3.

3.2   The Building Block Hypothesis

As an extension of the Schema Theorem, Goldberg introduced the Building Block Hypothesis [Goldberg, 1989]. Short, low order, highly fit schemata, which play such an important role in the standard genetic algorithm are given the name of *Building Blocks*. Since they represent highly fit schemata, the Schema Theorem predicts that they will be allocated increasingly more trials in following generations. When these building blocks are recombined into another single chromosome, its fitness is likely to increase as the chromosome combines the fitter parts of each of its parental chromosomes. The chromosomes created are enhanced, using the best partial solutions of previous chromosomes, eventually resulting in a global optimum. This is known as the Building Block Hypothesis.

First, a simple example is given. This indicates that the recombination of building blocks can indeed lead to an increase in fitness. Consider a problem, where each chromosome x consists of two integers: x_1 and x_2. Each represents a value between 0 and 3, and is coded with 2 bits. The fitness is given as $f(x) = (x_1)^2 + (x_2)^2$, resulting in a global optimum for $x_1 = x_2 = 3$. The following holds for the average fitness of the building block schemata:

- 1st order schemata:

$$f(1***) > f(0***)$$
$$f(*1**) > f(*0**)$$
$$f(**1*) > f(**0*)$$
$$f(***1) > f(***0)$$

- 2nd order schemata:

$$f(11**) > f(10**) > f(01**) > f(00**)$$
$$f(**11) > f(**10) > f(**01) > f(**00)$$

According to the Building Block Hypothesis, there is an expectation that the first order schemata with 1's will be selected in an increasing order and recombine into second order schemata. These will in turn be selected in an increasing order, and recombine to ultimately form the global optimum of $f(x) = 18$, represented by the string $x = (1\ 1\ 1\ 1)$.

The above problem can be classified as *non-deceptive*, as it leads the genetic algorithms towards the global optimum following the prediction of the Building Block Hypothesis. In contrast, consider the highly *deceptive* problem where the fitness value is given by:

$$f(x) = (x_1)^2 + (x_2)^2 \qquad \text{for } x_1, x_2 \neq 0$$
$$f(x) = 20 \qquad\qquad\quad \text{for } x_1 = x_2 = 0$$

Now, the equations for average fitness values of the first and second order schemata given above are all still valid (e.g., $f(1***) = 10$ and $f(0***) = 6.5$), but they lead the algorithm directly away from the global optimum of $x = (0\,0\,0\,0)$. The only possibility of finding this optimum is when it is generated by chance, either in the first population or by a lucky crossover or mutation, which becomes increasingly unlikely as the genetic algorithm progresses and a greater number of 1's find their way into the population.

But what happens when we change the fitness value of the problem again, into the following:

$$f(x) = (x_1)^2 + (x_2)^2 \qquad \text{for } x_1, x_2 \neq 0$$
$$f(x) = 1000 \qquad\qquad\quad \text{for } x_1 = x_2 = 0$$

None of the equations for average fitness values of the first and second order schemata given above remain valid (e.g., $f(1***) = 10$ and $f(0***) = 129$). In practice however, the algorithm will still be led away from the global optimum of $x = (0\,0\,0\,0)$ towards the local optimum of $x = (1\,1\,1\,1)$. Obviously, this contrasts with the predictions of the Building Block Hypothesis. In fact, the algorithm would find the global optimum only in the same cases as with the previous global optimum of 20, even though the BBH would suggest that the fitter building blocks (i.e. schemata with one '0' and three "don't cares") recombine and ultimately form the global optimum of $x = (0\,0\,0\,0)$.

This apparent clash between the Building Block Hypothesis and practice has led to the classification of the BBH into a *static* and a *dynamic* version. The Static Building Block Hypothesis [Grefenstette, 1993] is the version that has been described and used so far. It makes use of *static average fitness*, defined as the theoretical average fitness and calculated over all possible strings which belong to this particular schema (it is called 'static' since its value cannot change):

The *Static Building Block Hypothesis* (SBBH): Given any short, low order schema, a genetic algorithm is expected to converge to the schema with the best *static* average fitness.

Unfortunately this hypothesis is of limited practical value in that a genetic algorithm is unlikely to determine the theoretical average fitness of a schema, because in practice the limited sampling of schemata is always biased. Therefore, genetic algorithms in practice will follow the Dynamic Building Block Hypothesis [Spears, 1993]:

> The *Dynamic Building Block Hypothesis* (DBBH): Given any short, low order schema, a genetic algorithm is expected to converge to the schema with the best *dynamic* (observed) average fitness.

The dynamic average fitness is the fitness that is observed in the present population, and can therefore differ quite substantially from the static version. In other words: a genetic algorithm estimates the static average fitness from dynamic and biased sampling. The observed average fitness of a schema can be quite different from its theoretical counterpart, implying that the algorithm may not converge to the schema with the best static average fitness. This complies with the example given earlier where the global optimum, in spite of higher static fitness values, is not found if the string (0 0 0 0), which has such an impact on the values of the dynamic fitness averages, is not a member of the initial population or created by a very lucky crossover and/or mutation.

Finally, it can be concluded that the DBBH is more in accordance with the Schema Theorem, which also makes predictions based on the observed fitness values of the present population.

In reference to previous examples, it must be noted that these 'needle-in-a-haystack' problems are extremely difficult to optimise by any method besides exhaustively probing every possible solution. Even more than the genetic algorithm, any gradient-based search would immediately be led away from the optimum and end up in the local minimum.

Overview

There is no doubt that a genetic algorithm follows the Dynamic Building Block Hypothesis, however it depends on the error space of the particular problem, whether it is led towards the global optimum or not. When there is a large variance of the fitness within schemata, it will be highly unlikely that the dynamic fitness represents its static counterpart well, resulting in seemingly anomalous results. For the crossover operator to be of practical use, the chromosomal representation must be such that strong building blocks actually exist, with only small variances within the schemata. The solution to this situation, however, is not given by either the Schema Theorem or the Building Block Hypothesis.

3.3 The Walsh-Schema Transform

The Walsh-Schema Transform is an efficient, analytical method for predicting the expected performance of genetic algorithms. The Walsh transform of a function $f: x \rightarrow \mathbb{R}$, where x is a binary string of length l, is given by:

$$w_j = \frac{1}{2^l} \sum_{x=0}^{2^l-1} f(x)\psi_j(x) \text{ with } \quad \psi_j(x) = \prod_{i=1}^{l}(-1)^{x_i \cdot j_i}$$

where w_j = the Walsh coefficient relating to j, either +1 or –1,
  j = a binary string of length l,
  x_i = the value of the ith bit of x (0 or 1),
  j_i = the value of the ith bit of j (0 or 1).

The inverse Walsh function is defined as: $\quad f(x) = \sum_{j=0}^{2^l-1} w_j \cdot \psi_j(x)$

So for the case of a two bit string: $\quad f(x) = \pm w_{00} \pm w_{01} \pm w_{10} \pm w_{11}$.

The *Walsh-schema transform* is now defined as:

$$f(H) = \sum_{j=J(H)} w_j \cdot \psi_j(\beta(H))$$

where $J(H)$ is a set generator of schema H: $\quad J_i(H_i) = \begin{cases} 0, & \text{if } H_i = * \\ *, & \text{if } H_i = 0,1 \end{cases}$

and $\beta(H)$ maps H to a binary string: $\quad \beta_i(H_i) = \begin{cases} 0, & \text{if } H_i = 0,* \\ 1, & \text{if } H_i = 1 \end{cases}$

Using these definitions the average schema payoff function $f(H)$ of a schema H can be trans-formed into Walsh coefficients. For example: $f(**1) = w_{000} + w_{001}, f(**0) = w_{000} - w_{001}$, etc.

In the *static* version of this transform, Walsh coefficients are calculated for a fitness function $f(x)$ via this complex and computationally very expensive method. First, the average fitness of every possible schema with 1's and/or 'don't cares' must be calculated, for which all 2^l possible strings must be evaluated. The actual Walsh coefficients can be computed via the back-substitution algorithm of the fast Walsh transform, which requires $O(l \cdot 2^l)$

operations. Having completed this, the problem can be analysed by inspecting the values of the Walsh coefficients, giving some insight into the deceptiveness of the problem. Besides the computational effort already mentioned, this method requires a *flat population*, in which every single possible string is equally represented, rendering it of little value for practical problems.

New developments in this area include the development of the *nonuniform Walsh-Schema Transform*, that is no longer based on a flat population, but on a fixed-sized real-life nonuniform population. It requires a great deal less computational effort, since only the actual population requires evaluation, providing a dynamic analysis of medium sized problems for which the static version would be impractical [Bridges and Goldberg, 1993].

3.4   Markov Chain Analysis

Yet another approach to a fundamental theory of genetic algorithms is Markov chain analysis. As opposed to most models where certain approximations are necessary, Markov chains are useful in forming an exact model of genetic algorithms. This method is only appropriate on a small scale though, as the transition matrix used in the analysis grows exponentially with increasing population size and chromosome length. For any realistic genetic algorithm the transition matrix becomes of unmanageable size.

In the Markov chain analysis, every possible state the genetic algorithm can be in is defined, complete with probabilities *p(present state, next state)* of all the transitions the system can make to any other state, including the present state itself. These probabilities are retained in a transition matrix. A state defines the contents of every gene in every chromosome of the population. A schema *H*, as defined before, now occupies one or more states, depending upon the number of "don't cares" in that particular schema. All chromosomes in those occupied states are a member of that particular schema, and of course a state can be occupied by several schemata.

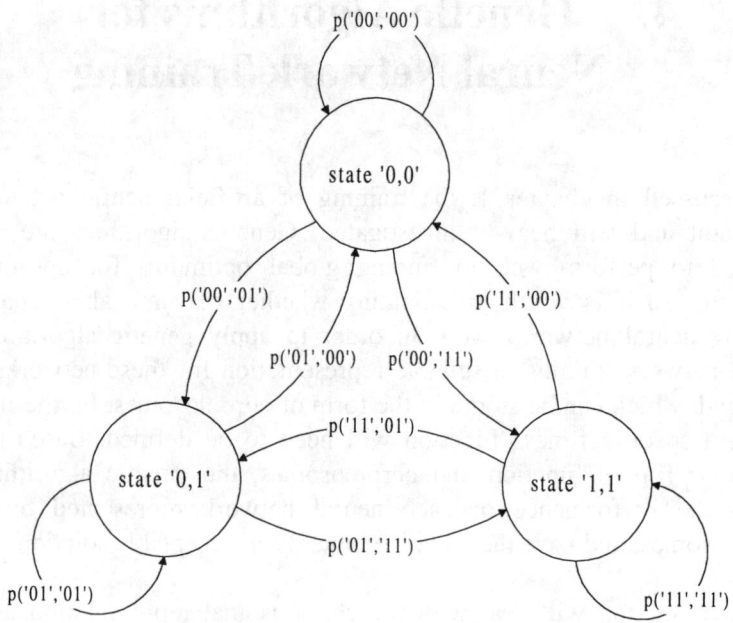

Figure 3.3   *Markov chain for a genetic algorithm with N=2 and l=1*

In figure 3.3 an example is given of a Markov chain for an algorithm with $N = 2$ (there are 2 chromosomes in the population) and $l = 1$ (each chromosomes consists of one gene). Here, state '0,1' signifies one chromosome of the population is equal to (0), and the other is equal to (1). Schema $H = \{\,0\,\}$ now occupies state '0,0', schema $H = \{\,1\,\}$ occupies state '1,1', and the last possible schema, $H = \{\,*\,\}$, occupies all three states.

For a population of size N with binary chromosomes of length l, the number of states equals $\begin{pmatrix} N + 2^l - 1 \\ N \end{pmatrix} = \dfrac{(N + 2^l - 1)!}{N!\,(2^l - 1)!}$, since the location of the chromosomes in the population is of no concern. For a relatively small genetic algorithm with 10 chromosomes of 10 bits each, the number of states would already become greater than $3.6 \cdot 10^{23}$, with more than $1.3 \cdot 10^{47}$ transition probabilities. Each state would be described by ten binary numbers of 10 bits each. Clearly, it would be impossible to manage such a great number of states and transition probabilities.

4. Genetic Algorithms for Neural Network Training

As discussed in chapter 1, the training of artificial neural networks is important and still heavily investigated. Genetic algorithms are widely claimed to perform well in finding global optimums for optimisation problems, so it is worth investigating whether they are also capable of training neural networks well. In order to apply genetic algorithms for neural network training, a suitable representation for these networks must be found, which can be stored in the form of chromosomes. Furthermore, a problem specific fitness function will need to be defined. Based on the particular fitness function and chromosomes, the genetic algorithm can assess the performance of each neural network represented by those chromosomes, and have them evolve towards an acceptable solution.

The next section will deal with the chromosomal representation and the corresponding fitness function of neural networks. Before the algorithm is run, several GA-specific parameters, as discussed in chapter 2, need to be set. Some of these parameters will be fixed to a certain option or value, others will be systematically altered in order to find the best settings for the problem at hand. This is described in section 4.2. In the last two sections, methods for improving the genetic algorithms will be discussed which are specific to the problem of learning the weights of a neural network. This is accomplished by applying and extending the theoretical concepts as discussed in the previous chapter.

4.1 Combining genetic algorithms and neural networks

The genetic algorithms and neural networks can be combined in several ways. So far, genetic algorithms have been mostly used to:
- generate the weights of a neural network,
- generate the architecture of a neural network,
- generate both the architecture and the weights of a neural network simultaneously,
- analyse a neural network.

When analysing neural networks, genetic algorithms are sometimes used to identify the input patterns that yield certain outputs for an existing neural network [Eberhart, 1992]. In this way, neural networks can be analysed to determine how they separate or cluster inputs, which can reveal important characteristics of the input patterns.

Generating the architecture of a neural network with or without simultaneously generating its weights, has proven to be a very difficult task, yielding only moderate results on relatively small problems. Every individual in the population codes a neural network structure, with or without its weights. During evaluation, a chromosome is first translated into a neural network structure. When the weights are not coded in the chromosome, initial weights are usually generated randomly. A training stage follows, generally being a fixed number of back-propagation steps (requiring a training set) or even a second genetic algorithm. Finally, a test set is used to determine the fitness of the network. Usually, the fitness function of the network incorporates a measure of the complexity of the particular network, in order to give the genetic algorithm a preference for smaller networks. At present, most of the research in this area looks at ways of efficiently coding a network structure into a chromosome in an attempt to simplify the optimisation problem. For some recent developments see e.g. [Maniezzo, 1994] and [Kitano, 1994].

We have used the genetic algorithm to train a neural network whose structure is predefined and remains fixed. This method provides an alternative to back-propagation (gradient descent) as described in chapter one, and has several advantages. For example, genetic algorithms do not require any error-gradient information. In contrast to algorithms like back-propagation, genetic algorithms can be used where this information is unavailable or is computationally expensive, or when the transfer function of the neurons is not differentiable or discontinuous. Furthermore, genetic algorithms can be used to train a wide variety of neural networks, including fully recurrent structures. Last but not least, genetic algorithms are presumed to perform a global search of the weight space and should therefore be less likely to become stuck in a local minimum than back-propagation, which pursues only a single route along the weight space. However, a disadvantage of training a neural network with a genetic algorithm is that it may be quite slow compared to back-propagation.

As this book investigates the application of generating the weights of a neural network using a genetic algorithm, the rest of this chapter will focus on this particular application. First, the manner in which neural network weights are stored in chromosomes is presented, followed by an explanation of the function used by the genetic algorithm to evaluate these chromosomes.

Chromosomal representation

Since the network structure, including the neuron's target function, is predefined and remains identical throughout the process of the genetic algorithm, it is not necessary to code any architectural information into the chromosome. Thus it is possible to define a network solely by its set of weights, in which the thresholds of the neurons are included. These real-valued weights need to be coded into the chromosome. Previously, this was accomplished by coding them into the string using a binary mechanism, due to the presumed superiority of binary genetic algorithms on which most research had been directed. These binary values represented integers, usually via a Gray coding which has better performance when genetic operators such as crossover or mutation are applied. When retrieving the information stored into a chromosome, the integers were translated into a range of real-valued weights. This procedure has the disadvantage that the weights can only be within a predefined range of values and with fixed precision.

Encouraging results have been reported using real-valued coding [Janikow and Michalewicz, 1991], and it has been shown that the presumed better behaviour of binary chromosomes had no real theoretical basis [Wright, 1991]. In fact, real-coded genetic algorithms have several advantages, including:

- Increased efficiency; bit strings do not need to be converted to and from real numbers for every function evaluation. Also, the genetic operators can be applied far less frequently as the number of genes in a chromosome has decreased significantly. In total, this could result in an overall ten-fold increase in execution speed.
- Increased precision; in a real number representation there is no loss of precision due to the binary representation. As a real-valued number is seen as one gene and an increase in the binary width of the number has therefore no influence on the functioning of the genetic algorithm whatsoever, apart from a higher precision and more memory usage of course.
- Greater freedom to use different mutation and crossover techniques based on the real representation; for instance, the 'linear crossover' operator calculates weighted averages of the parents' alleles.
- Better results; Hamming cliffs and other artefacts of bit mutation are avoided. It is also reported that floating point representation produces more consistent results from run to run [Janikow and Michalewicz, 1991].

For these reasons, real-valued coding has beeen used to store the weights on the chromosomes. Practical experience indicates that genetic algorithms obtain better results when parameters of the problem that are related to

Network

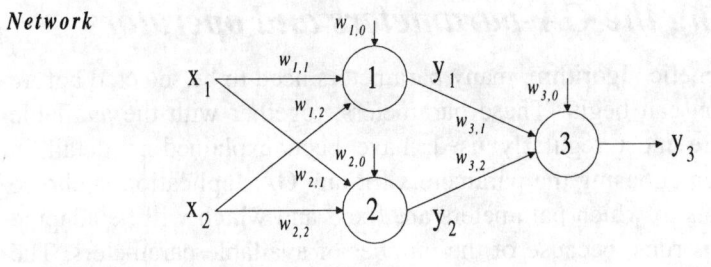

Chromosome

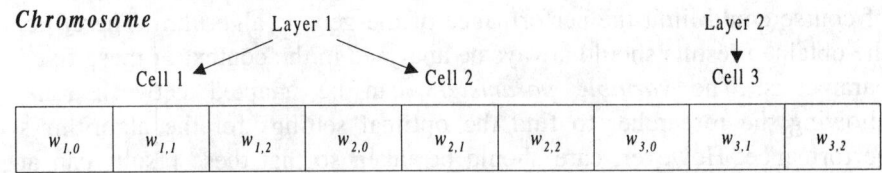

Figure 4.1   *Example showing how the weights of a neural network are coded into a chromosome*

each other, are also coded closer to each other on the chromosome. Therefore, all the weights of one neuron are coded next to each other, and the neurons are coded layer by layer. Refer figure 4.1 for a simple example. Of course, this systematic method of storing the weights also makes the process of storing and retrieving these values more efficient.

Fitness function

During the execution of the genetic algorithm, the fitness of every chromosome needs to be determined. For a particular chromosome, the network weights are restored from the chromosome, using the coding described above. Following this, the neural network is fully defined and tested using the normal procedure with a test set of input patterns and their target outputs. This test set can be identical to the training set for the back-propagation method. The network's outputs to each of the test patterns is calculated and compared to the target outputs, specified in the test set and the sum of the squared errors is calculated. After all test patterns have been fed to the network, these errors are summed into the total network error. Since this training error on the test set is a very good measure of how well the network performs, it can directly be used to calculate a fitness value. A form of inversion operation is required because a 'better' network has a lower training error, but needs to have a higher fitness value.

Since genetic algorithms strive to optimise the fitness value, chromosomes will be generated that code neural networks with increasingly lower training errors. This ensures that better and better networks will be generated, which is the goal of the entire process.

4.2   Setting the GA-parameters and operators

As with any genetic algorithm, many parameters need to be selected before the optimisation can begin. These parameters, together with the available options that are most regularly used, have been explained in detail in chapter 2. When choosing the parameters for any GA application, a choice must be made as to which parameters are fixed and which will be adapted between various runs, because of the number of available parameters. The *fixed parameters* should not be changed for any of the experiments, which of course could limit the performance of the genetic algorithm. Therefore, the obtained results should always be analysed in the context of these fixed parameters. The *variable parameters* can be adapted between runs, allowing the researcher to find the optimal settings for the algorithm's performance. However, care should be taken so that these results can at least be generalised for the problem at hand, meaning that enough runs with random initialisation must be completed to ensure that the obtained results are reliable. Preferably, the particular setting for which the algorithm performs best should be optimal for a whole category of problems (for example with certain neural network sizes) or even for all problems of this type, which in the context of this book is neural network learning. Then, the genetic algorithm can be said to have been optimised for neural network learning in general.

In this book, most parameters remain fixed, while the genetic operators of mutation and crossover are adapted. This is done because these latter genetic operators heavily influence the performance of the algorithm and therefore they are the most valuable candidates for a parametric study.

Normal parameters

These parameters are set in the common pattern of most researchers, making it easier to compare results with other reported research, if so desired. The settings are:

- Population: the population size has been set to 50, which is often used for genetic algorithms as a trade-off between the time to convergence and the fitness value of the final result. It is found that smaller populations generally converge faster, but they find the global optimum less frequently. Larger populations have the opposite characteristics.
- Initialisation: since each gene represents a neural network weight, which usually has a low value, a random *Gaussian* weight initialisation is chosen with a mean of 0 and a standard deviation of 5. This ensures most weights are between −5 and +5, while occasionally allowing for higher values (smaller than −10 or larger than +10).

- Fitness normalisation: in order to maintain constant selective pressure as the algorithm progresses and the fitness values are closer together, a *ranking* mechanism is used that ranks the chromosomes in order of fitness. Completed in *reverse*, it accommodates for the fact that low network error values should represent high fitness values. A *bias* of 10 is applied, resulting in a fitness value for the best chromosome which is 10 times higher than that of the worst chromosome.
- Selection: the standard *roulette* selection mechanism is used.
- Replacement: every newly generated chromosome is *unconditionally* inserted into the population of the next generation. Two chromosomes are always created at the same time from two parents. So, the replacement type is children replacing their parents. In every generation all chromosomes are replaced, except for the best performing chromosome, which is retained and inserted into the next generation without change (*elitism*).

Mutation operator

In this genetic algorithm where genes represent real numbers, the chosen mutation type is *Gaussian addition*, adding a random number to the mutated value. The standard deviation of this number is equal to 1, with a mean of 0. These parameters are fixed and therefore remain unchanged during the various experiments. The mutation rate is chosen to be variable, ranging from 0.1 (mutate only 10% of the genes of the offspring) to 1.0 (always mutate) per gene and adapted with a step size of 0.1. The mutation rates are quite high compared to those used for simpler binary GAs, however initial experiments exploring the region of interest indicated these settings produced the best results. When mutation is performed on a small binary chromosome, it has a very high impact since the gene in question is switched to its opposite state. For real-valued chromosomes however, the addition of a probabilistic value is far less disruptive and therefore warrants a higher mutation rate.

Crossover operator

Even more than the mutation operator, the crossover type used in the experiments determines to a high degree how successful the genetic algorithm will be in finding optimal solutions. The most frequently used crossover types are explained in chapter 3, however the potential range is almost endless. The types *1-point* crossover, *2-point* crossover and *uniform* crossover are further investigated in this chapter. These crossover types are subsequently varied between a crossover rate of 0.1 (apply crossover to 10% of the offspring) and 1.0 (always apply crossover), again with steps of 0.1.

Experiments

The results of experimental studies into the effects of varying crossover and mutation parameters are presented in the next chapter.

In order to keep computing simulation time to a manageable level, not all combinations of parameters described above have been used. Instead, the (less influential) mutation rate is adapted while the crossover type and rate are fixed at a type or value which has been shown by initial experiments to perform relatively well (2-point crossover, applied with rate 0.8). The mutation rate is fixed at the (semi-)optimal level found by the experiments, after which follow the rest of the simulations (investigating the various crossover types and rates).

Once the final parameters (mutation and crossover rates) are set at an appropriate value, other problems with increasing network sizes can be dealt with. These problems include the classification of iris flowers (refer section 5.2), interpreting the dots on a dice as a number (refer section 5.3), an analysis of medical data relating to heart problems (refer section 5.4) and the classification of ships (refer section 5.5). It is important to note there are several reasons for retaining fixed and possibly sub-optimal GA-settings throughout these latter experiments. The increasing network sizes cause the simulation times to grow exponentially, making it virtually impossible to perform exhaustive parametric studies for medium and larger problems. Furthermore, it is important to find a general setting for the genetic parameters which gives a reasonable performance for a multitude of neural networks, so the investigator is not required to endlessly experiment with parameters. It is of greater importance in the future, that a given neural network can be reliably trained by a single genetic algorithm within a certain time span.

4.3   Introducing a new crossover operator

In genetic algorithms, the crossover operator performs a very important task. It is a very powerful operator, without which there simply would not be any 'real' genetic algorithms, since it is the only possible form of exchange of information between the chromosomes of a population. In general, two very important factors need to be recognised when dealing with crossover:

1. Crossover is required to combine partial information from several chromosomes into one superior solution. It combines lower order building blocks into new, higher order building blocks. This effect of crossover is essential to the functioning of the algorithm, and considers crossover as a *constructive* operator.
2. Crossover can also very easily disrupt the effective building blocks that have been previously formed. Crossover is consequently also a *disruptive* operator, whose effect must be limited. Refer to section 3.1 for more information on the disruptive behaviour of crossover.

These two 'functions' of crossover are contradictory, often resulting in a trade-off, either by selecting multi-point (or uniform) crossover with a relatively low crossover rate, or 2-point crossover with a higher crossover rate.

In genetic algorithms for neural network training a further difficulty arises because the weights are very much dependent upon each other. In other words: setting one weight to a better value may have minimal or no effect unless the other weights of that particular neuron are also set to their appropriate values, making it possible for the neuron to perform an effective separation of its input space and so forming a useful hyperplane. Furthermore, the important relation between weights belonging to the same neuron also makes it very unlikely that selecting some weights from one chromosome and the other weights from another chromosome would result in successful neuron operation. This 'intra-crossing' of neurons has already been limited by the manner in which the cell-weights are coded onto the chromosomes, locating all weights of a neuron next to each other. This has been illustrated by the example for the effect of crossover in section 3.1, where schema $H_1 = \{ * 1\ 0 * * * * * \}$ had a far greater chance of surviving the crossover operator than schema $H_2 = \{ * 1 * * * * 0 * \}$, due to its smaller defining length. By setting the weights of a neuron next to each other on the chromosome, the defining length of this group is limited to the actual number of weights.

However, by eliminating all possibilities of selecting a crossover point within such a weight group, the reduction in neuron disruption could be

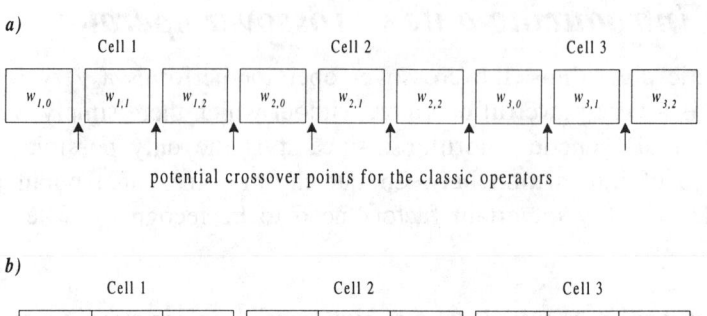

potential crossover points for the classic operators

potential crossover points for the NN-specific operators

Figure 4.2   *Example of the difference in potential crossover points*

eliminated. This is the basis for our new crossover operator which has been designed specifically for training neural networks. With this *neural network specific crossover operator*, previously evolved neurons cannot be disrupted by crossover, whereas neurons from the available chromosomes remain free to be combined by the same operator. Apart from one paper, where a similar concept was mentioned together with some other experimental operators [Montana, 1991], no such neural network specific crossover operator has been used and published to the best of our knowledge. Montana reported no benefit from his crossover operator, but due to the lack of actual parameter values or the number of separate runs completed, those results could not be replicated and we have found significant benefits from a network-specific crossover operator.

Taking the simple network of figure 4.1, various potential crossover points for the different crossover operators are shown in figure 4.2: (a) for the classic *n*-point and uniform crossover operators and (b) for the NN-specific versions.

An example of a NN-specific crossover type is given in figure 4.3. Two chromosomes, representing the neural networks A and B, have been selected as the parents for crossover. The neural network consists of three hidden neurons and two output neurons. The NN-specific crossover operator determines the potential crossover points (as shown in figure 4.2), that lie in between the weights groups of the various neuron cells. Then, it selects the points which will actually be used for crossover. A uniform NN-specific crossover operator would certainly select more points for this than a 2-point NN-specific crossover operator. After the crossover operation is

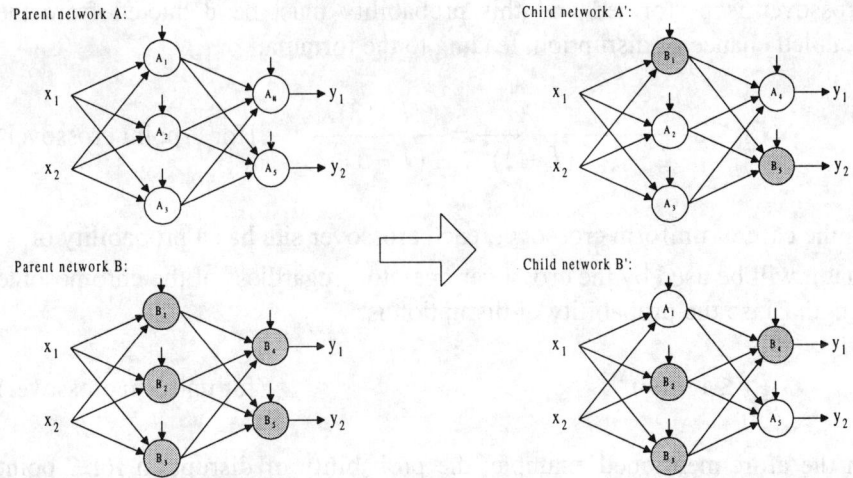

Figure 4.3 *Example of a NN-specific crossover operation (phenotypes)*

performed, two child chromosomes will be generated representing networks A' and B', that consist of neuron cells taken as a whole from the parental networks.

Consider an output neuron of the networks in figure 4.3, that clearly demonstrates that the possibility of disruption of the neuron is quite large if the crossover operator is not NN-specific. In total, a chromosome coding this network needs $3 \cdot 3 + 2 \cdot 4 = 17$ genes. Each output neuron occupies four of these genes. For 1-point crossover, one crossover point is selected in the chromosome. The probability that this crossover point will fall in between weights of a particular output neuron is equal to $\dfrac{4-1}{17-1} = 0.1875$ (of the 17 – 1 potential crossover points, 4 – 1 could lead to disruption). Generally, for a neuron with X inputs coded into a chromosome of length L, the probability of disruption with 1-point crossover is (upper bound since the two chromosomes could have genes in common):

$$P_d \le \frac{X}{L-1} \qquad\qquad \text{(for 1-point crossover)}$$

When 2-point crossover is used as opposed to 1-point, this probability is multiplied by two, due to the fact that if any of these crossover points lies in the specified neuron weight group disruption occurs. When the two crossover points coincide on one and the same crossover site within the neuron's weight group, the disruption is reduced. In that case, no actual crossover is performed and this probability must be deducted from the doubled chance of disruption, leading to the formula:

$$P_d \leq 2 \cdot \frac{X}{L-1} - \frac{X}{(L-1)^2} = \frac{(2L-3)X}{(L-1)^2} \qquad \text{(for 2-point crossover)}$$

In the case of uniform crossover, each crossover site has a probability of $\frac{1}{2}$ that it will be used by the crossover operator (regardless of the chromosome length L), so the probability of disruption is:

$$P_d \leq 1 - (\tfrac{1}{2})^X \qquad \text{(for uniform crossover)}$$

In the afore-mentioned example, the probability of disruption for 2-point crossover is equal to $\dfrac{(2 \cdot 17 - 3)3}{(17-1)^2} \approx 0.363$, and equal to $1 - (\tfrac{1}{2})^3 = 0.875$ for uniform crossover, assuming the two chromosomes have no genes in common. These disruption chances are indeed quite large, and will therefore make the survival of a particular neuron weight group over several generations very unlikely. Of course, these probabilities of disruption are always zero for the NN-specific crossover operators, due to their purposely built-in protection of neuron weight groups. The only way in which a neuron can then be lost, is if a particular chromosome is not selected at all by the algorithm for reproduction due to poor relative performance of the related network.

In larger networks, the probabilities of disruption for a specific neuron reduce somewhat, simply because the fixed number of crossover points are spread over a larger chromosome (of course, this does not hold for uniform crossover). For instance, consider a neuron with 10 inputs, that is part of a network with a total of $L = 200$ network weights, then the chances of disruption become:

$$P_d = 0.0503 \qquad \text{(1-point crossover)}$$
$$P_d = 0.1003 \qquad \text{(2-point crossover)}$$
$$P_d = 0.9990 \qquad \text{(uniform crossover)}$$

Therefore, it can be expected the 1-point and 2-point crossover operators will begin to demonstrate behaviour that is similar to the NN-specific versions as the network increases in size. Normal uniform crossover however, increases the chance of disruption as the number of inputs to a neuron grows.

Clearly, the NN-specific crossover operators have the disadvantage that, with the elimination of potential crossover points within a neuron's weight group, the possibility of forming new useful hyperplanes by crossover has been eliminated. After all, crossover can no longer combine parts of several neural weight groups into a new group. However, it is expected that the advantages of the lack of disruption will outweigh this disadvantage, since the experiments of the previous paragraph (see also the results presented in chapter 5) indicate the dominant search method is genetic hill-climbing, where the mutation operator is used to optimise the various weights or hyperplanes. The mutation and crossover operators gracefully work together, with mutation optimising the neuron weights and crossover subsequently recombining them into better networks.

4.4   Avoiding the loss of useful genetic material

The Building Block Hypothesis (refer section 3.2) states that genetic algorithms work well when short, low-order, highly fit schemata recombine to form even more highly fit higher order schemata. The ability to form fitter and fitter partial solutions by combining building blocks is therefore believed to be a primary source of the GA's power. However, despite the presumed central role of building blocks and recombination, a precise and quantitative description of how schemata interact and combine during a typical evolution of a GA search, has to date not been reported in literature.

The Royal Road function

Research into the formation of building blocks can be accomplished by isolating fitness landscape features implied by the Building Block Hypothesis, and studying in detail the GA's behaviour on simple landscapes containing those features. In [Forrest and Mitchell, 1993], a *Royal Road function* is constructed. This Royal Road function features short, low-order, highly fit schemata, medium-order higher fitness schemata that can result from combinations of the low-order schemata, and that in turn can combine to create even higher fitness schemata. These schemata, known as stepping stones, should lead the genetic algorithm towards the global optimum of the proposed landscape.

The proposed binary Royal Road function is a simple one: a string of 64 bits is divided into eight consecutive parts of eight bits each. Each of these 8-bit parts form an order-8 schema, filled with eight 1's and "don't cares" for the rest. If a bit string x belongs to such an order-8 schema, eight points are added to its fitness. Similarly, four order-16 schemata are formed, potentially awarding x with 16 extra points to its fitness. Finally, two order-32 schemata give 32 points. The total fitness of a bit string x is calculated by summing all the fitness contributions of the schemata to which x belongs. The schemata H_1 to H_{14} and their respective contributions c_1 to c_{14} are shown in table 4.1. For example, the bit string

$$x = (\ 11101000 \quad 11111111 \quad 00000000 \quad 11100011 \quad 11111111 \quad 11111111 \quad 10100011 \quad 10111111\ )$$

belongs to schemata H_2, H_5, H_6 and H_{11}, so its fitness equals $c_2 + c_5 + c_6 + c_{11} = 40$. The optimal string of all 1's belongs to all schemata and would thus receive a total fitness of 192.

Table 4.1   *The proposed Royal Road function*

Schema	Fitness
$H_1 = \{$ 11111111** $\}$	$c_1 = 8$
$H_2 = \{$ ********11111111** $\}$	$c_2 = 8$
$H_3 = \{$ ****************11111111** $\}$	$c_3 = 8$
$H_4 = \{$ ************************11111111******************************** $\}$	$c_4 = 8$
$H_5 = \{$ ********************************11111111************************ $\}$	$c_5 = 8$
$H_6 = \{$ **11111111**************** $\}$	$c_6 = 8$
$H_7 = \{$ **11111111******** $\}$	$c_7 = 8$
$H_8 = \{$ **11111111 $\}$	$c_8 = 8$
$H_9 = \{$ 1111111111111111** $\}$	$c_9 = 16$
$H_{10} = \{$ ****************1111111111111111******************************** $\}$	$c_{10} = 16$
$H_{11} = \{$ ********************************1111111111111111**************** $\}$	$c_{11} = 16$
$H_{12} = \{$ **1111111111111111 $\}$	$c_{12} = 16$
$H_{13} = \{$ 11111111111111111111111111111111******************************** $\}$	$c_{13} = 32$
$H_{14} = \{$ ********************************11111111111111111111111111111111 $\}$	$c_{14} = 32$

Results

The experiments with Royal Road functions using 1-point crossover, indicated that in contrast to the expectations, the genetic algorithm experiences difficulty in finding the optimal string. Careful examinations of the intermediate populations showed the densities of the various schemata at each generation. Each time an order-8 schema was formed by the GA in one of the total of 128 members of the population, it spread out quickly to a density of about 95% of the pool. Identical phenomena occurred when a higher order schema was formed. However, the extra rewards, in the form of schemata H_9 to H_{14}, did lead the genetic algorithm to favour the higher order schemata at the cost of other lower order ones. For example, suppose that schemata H_1 and H_3 are present in 95% of the population, and no other schemata have yet been found. Further, suppose that a string x exists that only belongs to schema H_1, and thus not to schema H_3. If, for example by a lucky mutation, string x also suddenly belongs to schema H_2 and therefore schema H_9, its fitness will rise steeply from 8 to 32. This will cause the genetic algorithm to heavily favour this string x over all other strings of the population in its selection procedure, and the newly found higher order schema will spread quickly over the rest of the population. However, this causes the third 8-bit group of string x to simultaneously spread over the rest of the population, heavily reducing the previously high density of schema H_3 in the population. In other words: the sub-string of the third block of string x, which contained some 0's, drove out many of the previously existing instances of schema H_3 in the population. This phenomenon has been called *hitch-hiking*, since the 0's of the sub-string in question travelled alongside the highly-fit schema.

Forrest and Mitchell could not find a remedy or satisfying explanation for this disappointing behaviour of the genetic algorithm in the Royal Road function. Their hypothesis was that hitch-hiking occurred in the loci that were spatially adjacent to the high-fitness schemata (e.g., H_9 in the example above). In an attempt to reduce this effect, a new function was constructed that was functionally equivalent to the one described previously, however the strings were increased in length by inserting groups of eight *'s between the functional sub-groups of 8-bit blocks of 1's. This resulted in strings of 120 bits, of which 56 (the newly inserted sub-groups) were not functionally used. The idea being that a potentially damaging hitch-hiker would be at least 8 bits away from the schema on which it was hitch-hiking, and would thus likely be lost under crossover. However, the results with this new function were not significantly different from their previous results.

The hitch-hiking phenomenon

Explanation of the above results is based on the theoretical foundation of genetic algorithms as presented in chapter three. The use of 1-point crossover caused the high instance of hitch-hiking, as it is likely that the bits adjacent to the high-order schema are not separated from their close neighbours. After all, only 1 crossover point is chosen somewhere in the string of 64 bits, so on average, half the string, 32 bits, would be allowed to hitch-hike with the highly-fit schema to one of the two offspring. This explains the high degree of hitch-hiking of the initial Royal Road function. The remainder of the string, together with the complementary part of the other (weaker) parental string, would end up as the second (weaker) offspring. This is demonstrated in figure 4.4.

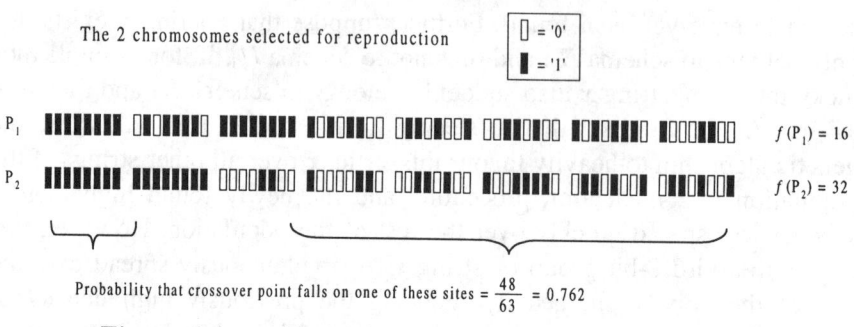

Probability that crossover point falls on one of these sites $= \dfrac{48}{63} = 0.762$

Figure 4.4   *Example of the hitch-hiking phenomenon*

When the single crossover site is chosen, there is a probability of 76.2% that the third sub-group of parent P_2 will hitch-hike with the same parent's highly fit first two sub-groups. This reduces the probability of forming a fitter child chromosome containing the first two sub-groups of parent P_2 and the third sub-group of parent P_1, that would have a fitness of 40. Furthermore, there is the added probability that one of the highly fit sub-groups is broken up by the crossover operation (disruption).

By introducing the sub-groups of eight *'s each between the functional groups, the length of the strings is increased to 120 bits. There is a reasonable possibility now that the crossover point will fall somewhere in the sub-groups ($\frac{79}{119} = 52.9\%$). However, this will not have a great effect on the degree of hitch-hiking of the functional bits. On average, half the string, which is now 60 bits long, would be allowed to hitch-hike. The only effect introduced is that the functional sub-groups are less likely to be broken up by the crossover operator. Previously, there were 63 potential crossover sites, of which 56 would cause one of the eight 8-bit groups to split up. Now, there are 119 potential crossover sites, of which still 56 would cause a split-up. The chance of a group being broken has fallen from 0.889 to 0.471. This should have some beneficial influence on the genetic algorithm, since the 1-point crossover operator has become less disruptive. Compare this with the introduction of the NN-specific crossover operator in the previous section, where the proposed limitation of the number of crossover sites is essentially equal to inserting an infinite number of genes in between the functional genes, causing the probability of disruption to fall to zero.

A method which would have counteracted the observed hitch-hiking phenomenon to some degree, uses a crossover operator with more crossover sites: n-point crossover with $n \geq 2$. This would reduce the number of adjacent bits expected to travel with the highly fit schema, since the string is broken up into a greater number of shorter sections. It is still expected that half the string would be allowed to form one offspring, and the other half would form the second offspring. Everything considered, each offspring is completely built of parts from the two parental strings (before mutation is applied). However, the probability of hitch-hiking has decreased slightly for the adjacent bits, and increased slightly for the bits which are further away from the highly fit schema. This results in a more even distribution of the various bits over the two offspring.

A more even probability of hitch-hiking for all bits of the string will increase with the used number of crossover points. An extreme is formed by the uniform crossover operator, where each bit would have a probability of 0.5 of travelling with the highly fit schema. Hitch-hiking is then not favoured any more, and can be regarded as non-existent. It can be concluded that hitch-hiking is only a problem when its probability is greater than 0.5.

The problem of hitch-hiking 0's can be solved by increasing the number of crossover points, although at the great cost of an extremely high disruption rate. In the worst case, the probability that a highly fit 16-bit schema is not disrupted during uniform crossover is equal to $\left(\frac{1}{2}\right)^{15} = 3.052 \cdot 10^{-5}$ (using the formula of section 4.3). In other words: one problem is solved at the expense of introducing an even greater problem.

The above can also be presented from a more mathematical point of view, by calculating the actual probabilities of hitch-hiking and disruption for the various crossover operators, based on the illustration of figure 4.4. In this case, useful probabilities are:
- the probability of disruption of the highly fit order-16 block,
- the probability of disruption of the fit order-8 block,
- the probability that the complete third sub-group of parent P_2 hitch-hikes with the order-16 block, and
- the probability that an optimal child with a fitness of 40 is formed.

These probabilities are calculated for 1-point, 2-point and uniform crossover, and their 'NN-specific' counterparts that only allow crossover sites in between the 8-bit sub-groups. The results can be seen in table 4.2.

Table 4.2   *Probabilities of various results by crossover*
operations, based on figure 4.4

Crossover operator	P(disruption of order-16 block)	P(disruption of order-8 block)	P(hitch-hiking of P_2's 3rd sub-group)	P(optimal child)
1-point	11.1%	11.1%	76.2%	1.6%
2-point	20.3%	20.7%	58.4%	2.4%
uniform	75%	96.9%	N/A	0.39%
NN-1-point	0%	0%	85.7%	14.3%
NN-2-point	0%	0%	75.5%	24.5%
NN-uniform	0%	0%	50%	50%

These figures indicate the impact of hitch-hiking reduces as the number of crossover points increases. At the same time though, the probabilities of disruption of the order-8 or order-16 blocks increases dramatically. The latter effect is stronger for higher n's (in n-point crossover), resulting in lower chances for the formation of an optimal child chromosome as the number of crossover points increases. Table 4.2 shows this is not yet the case for 2-point crossover, however it will become so, as n increases. For the NN-specific versions, no disruption is possible. This gives the increased number of crossover points the chance to reduce the hitch-hiking effect and thus increase the chances of an optimal child chromosome, as can be observed in table 4.2.

The reverse hitch-hiking phenomenon

Just as some genes in a chromosome can have a high chance, greater than 0.5, of hitch-hiking with an highly fit sub-group, others can have a low chance, smaller than 0.5. These genes are then likely to be separated from the highly fit sub-group, which may possibly be damaging if they are also beneficial to the chromosome's fitness. This phenomenon can be called *reverse hitch-hiking* and an example is illustrated in figure 4.5.

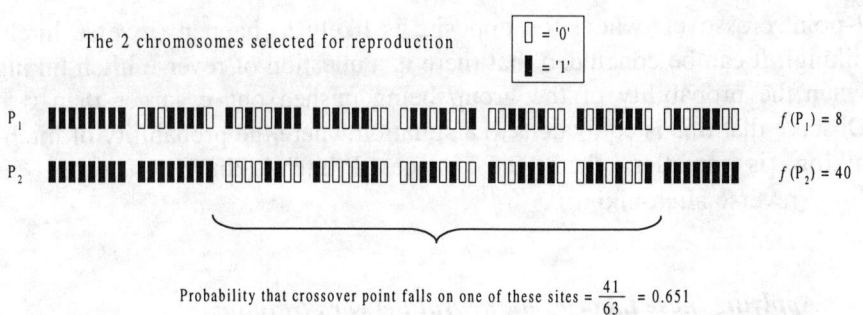

Probability that crossover point falls on one of these sites $= \dfrac{41}{63} = 0.651$

Figure 4.5   *Example of the reverse hitch-hiking phenomenon*

If 1-point crossover is applied to these parental chromosomes, the probability that the last sub-group of chromosome P_2 is separated from that parent's highly-fit order-16 block is 65.1%. In order words: the last sub-group of parent P_1 is likely to push its rival out of the highly fit child chromosome, so reducing its fitness to 32. In order to fully assess this situation, a table similar to table 4.2 is provided (refer table 4.3).

Table 4.3   *Probabilities of various results by crossover operations, based on figure 4.5*

Crossover operator	P(disruption of order-16 block)	P(disruption of order-8 block)	P(pushing out of P_2's last sub-group)	P(optimal child)
1-point	11.1%	11.1%	65.1%	12.7%
2-point	20.3%	20.6%	16.5%	45.1%
uniform	75%	93.8%	N/A	0.78%
NN-1-point	0%	0%	85.7%	14.3%
NN-2-point	0%	0%	24.5%	75.5%
NN-uniform	0%	0%	50%	50%

The various percentages in this table show the probabilities of the highly fit order-8 sub-group of parent P_2 being pushed out of the chromosome, reduce when 2-point crossover is used instead of 1-point. This is because the 2-point crossover has an even number of crossover points, breaking the strings up in three parts. Obviously, the first and last part of each parent chromosome will end up in the same child chromosome. Therefore, there is a larger probability that the highly fit sub-groups of parent P_2, situated at both ends of the chromosome, will travel together to the same child (hitch-hiking), resulting in an optimal child. This is in contrast to the situation for

1-point crossover, where the opposite is likely to happen (reverse hitch-hiking). It can be concluded that there is a question of reverse hitch-hiking when the probability of the group being pushed out is larger than 0.5. Observe that this is equivalent to a situation where the probability of hitch-hiking is smaller than 0.5, since P(hitch-hiking) is equal to 1 − P(reverse hitch-hiking).

Applying these theories on neural network training

Evidently, there is a high similarity between the proposed Royal Road function and any neural network weight optimisation problem. In both problems, some sub-groups exist within the chromosomes that are highly dependent on each other, and able to give the fitness value a boost if they attain the proper values. Therefore, it is to be expected that a genetic algorithm, training a neural network, will also suffer from the hitch-hikers and reverse hitch-hikers problem.

A crossover operation can have several harmful consequences, as has been shown in the present and previous chapters. First of all, crossover operations can cause *disruption* of a highly fit schema. Secondly, some crossover operators are biased towards disrupting some schemata on the basis of their defining length. If this is the case, the crossover operator is said to suffer from *representational bias*. Finally, the phenomena of (*reverse*) *hitch-hiking* can occur to some degree. In order to see to what degree the various crossover operators suffer from these effects, an assessment has been made in table 4.4 for 1-point, 2-point and uniform crossover.

Table 4.4   *Occurrence of various deleterious effects due to classic crossover operators*

Crossover operator	Representational bias of disruption	Probability of neuron disruption	Occurrence of (reverse) hitch-hiking
1-point	high	low	high
2-point	medium	medium	medium
uniform	nil	very high	nil

Table 4.4 shows that 1-point crossover suffers to a high degree from representational bias and the (reverse) hitch-hiking phenomena, while uniform crossover has a very high neuron disruption rate. The 2-point

crossover operator shows medium effects in all three areas, which accounts for its generally better performance in practical applications.

It is possible to overcome both the problem of (reverse) hitch-hiking and the problem of neuron disruption, by combining the proposed neural network specific crossover with uniform crossover. The neurons are then protected from disruption by the fact that only crossover sites between neuron groups may be chosen, so there is no danger of increased disruption by using the uniform version of this operator. Due to the uniform crossover of the various neuron groups, the problem of (reverse) hitch-hiking neuron groups is also solved. From above discussion it is clear that one can expect a better performance from NN-specific uniform crossover operator than from the NN-specific *n*-point operators. This can also be seen if a table similar to table 4.4 is provided for the NN-specific versions of 1-point, 2-point and uniform crossover (refer table 4.5).

Table 4.5   *Occurrence of various deleterious effects due to NN-specific crossover operators*

Crossover operator	Representational bias of disruption	Probability of neuron disruption	Occurrence of (reverse) hitch-hiking
NN-1-point	high	nil	high
NN-2-point	medium	nil	medium
NN-uniform	nil	nil	nil

The only difference between the two tables is the fact that the NN-specific character of the crossover operators prevents all instances of neuron disruption. From table 4.5 it is clear that NN-specific uniform crossover indeed does not suffer from any of these deleterious effects, rendering this crossover operator, at least in theory, the best option for neural network training.

5. Case-studies

The experimental results of five case-studies are presented in this chapter. The initial simulations of the exclusive OR problem are described in depth, as they will provide the settings that are also be used for the other problems. Various other problems will then be solved, with increasing network sizes and number of input patterns. This strategy aims to evaluate the improvements made to the genetic algorithm and to determine if they are able to scale up to bigger problems. Refer table 5.1 for a summary of the case-studies, each of which will be further explained in their respective sections.

Table 5.1   *Case-studies and their attributes*

Section	Case-study	Network size	No. of test patterns
5.1	Continuous exclusive OR	$2 * 4 * 2$	8
5.2	Iris flower classification	$4 * 4 * 3$	75
5.3	Dice classification	$9 * 6 * 6$	9
5.4	Heart disease classification	$13 * 10 * 1$	100
5.5	Ship classification	$17 * 12 * 12$	120

5.1   The 'continuous exclusive-OR' problem

The continuous exclusive-OR (XOR) problem is a standard problem and is often used as a test for neural network learning algorithms, as it is fairly difficult for a neural network to learn. It consists of a two-dimensional input space, as depicted in figure 5.1. This version of the XOR problem is called 'continuous' since the input values are not limited to binary values, but are allowed to take any value in a range, which in this case is between −1 and +1 (except for the value 0 which would be ambiguous). Each of these input vectors must be mapped into one of two possible categories (here called A and B) by the neural network. For this, two input neurons are used, four hidden neurons, and two output neurons.[1] The input neurons have a linear transfer function, simply copying the input to the output, and

---

[1] Two output neurons are used here to comply with the followed standard of one output neuron for each possible output class. In theory, one output neuron could suffice in a case such as this, with only two output classes, simply by mapping all vectors of class A to the output of value 0 and all vectors of class B to the output of value 1, or vice versa.

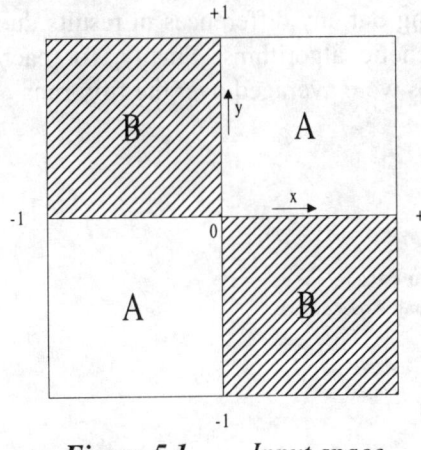

Figure 5.1   *Input space*

Table 5.2		Training data	
Input vectors		**Target vectors**	
x	*y*	*Class A*	*Class B*
0.2	0.5	1	0
0.5	0.2	1	0
-0.2	0.5	0	1
-0.5	0.2	0	1
-0.2	-0.5	1	0
-0.5	-0.2	1	0
0.2	-0.5	0	1
0.5	-0.2	0	1

act therefore as a buffer or input visualisation. The neurons in the following layers (hidden layer and output layer) have a sigmoid transfer function, and also deploy a threshold weight (with a constant input of 1) besides weighting all their inputs.

A network with four hidden neurons is used, since this is the minimum number required for a neural network to be able to solve a continuous XOR problem (as opposed to the two hidden neurons needed for the binary XOR problem). Each output vector represents the membership of the present input vector of one class, ranging between 0 (not a member of this class) and 1 (a full member of this class). The target values are either 0 or 1, as shown in table 5.2 where the training data is listed. Only two samples from each quadrant are used, in order to speed up the computations.

Results using the classic crossover operators

The experiments mentioned in section 4.2 are computed and analysed here. First, some experiments were completed to establish a satisfactory value for the mutation rate. Following this, the found mutation rate was fixed for the subsequent simulations with the 1-point, 2-point and uniform crossover operator. In all of these simulations, the genetic algorithm was run for 250 generations. For each generation, the network error of the best performing (i.e. fittest) chromosome of the pool of 50 was retained. The entire process was completed fifty times, each time starting with a different random initial population in order to avoid drawing conclusions based on a single 'lucky' or 'unlucky' result. In fact, the randomness was controlled with known seed numbers to ensure that it was possible to regenerate an identical initial population. This was used so that each experiment would begin with the same fifty initial populations, cancelling out any differences in results due to different starting points of the genetic algorithms. Finally, for each generation the best network error values were averaged over the fifty runs.

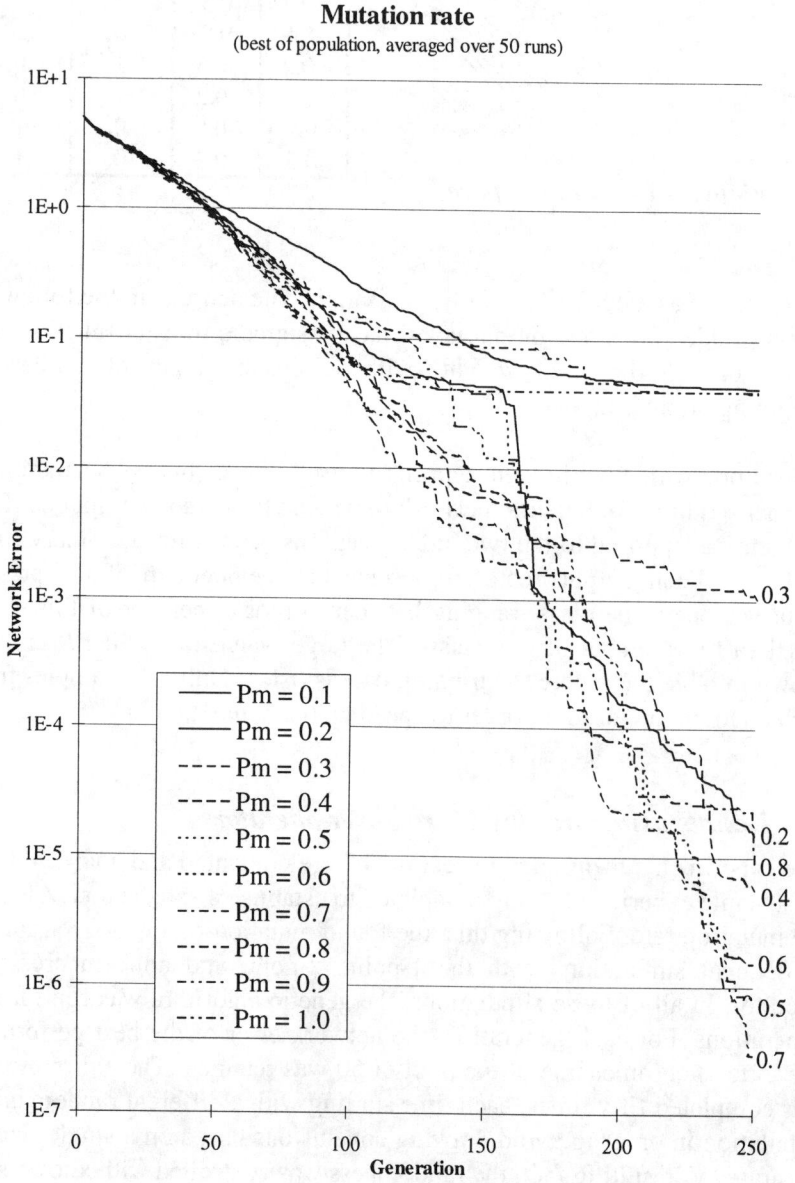

Figure 5.2   *Results with variable mutation rate (XOR problem)*

- **Mutation rate**

Early experiments indicated that relatively good results could be obtained using 2-point crossover with an applied rate of 0.8 when considering the network errors of the fittest chromosomes of the fifty populations after both 100 and 250 generations. Also, from a theoretical point of view (see section 3.1) 2-point crossover promised to give the best results of the classic crossover operators, based on its lower amount of disruption of building blocks. It was chosen not to use a NN-specific crossover operator here, to avoid the need for optimisation of the mutation rate for these special crossover operators, which could lead to biased results in further experiments. Therefore, the 2-point crossover operator, with $p_c = 0.8$, was utilised as a basis for the investigation towards the mutation operator. As noted before, fifty runs were completed for each setting of the mutation rate. In each of these runs the genetic algorithms was executed for 250 generations. The mutation rate was altered from $p_m = 0.1$ up to $p_m = 1.0$, with a step size of 0.1. A graph of the results is included as figure 5.2, and the results after 100 and 250 generations are repeated in table 5.3.

Table 5.3   *Resulting network error for each mutation rate*

Gen.	Mutation rate p_m									
	0.1	*0.2*	*0.3*	*0.4*	*0.5*	*0.6*	*0.7*	*0.8*	*0.9*	*1.0*
100	0.271	0.097	0.064	0.068	0.136	0.071	0.048	0.040	0.163	0.066
250	4.2E-2	1.5E-5	1.0E-3	5.7E-6	7.5E-7	1.5E-6	2.9E-7	8.6E-6	4.0E-2	4.0E-2

It follows that the best results were obtained using the higher mutation rates from 0.4 to 0.8. These rates are relatively high, compared to the values of 0.01 to 0.1 which are often used successfully by scientists for simpler genetic algorithms (e.g., algorithms with small binary chromosomes). Reasons for this relatively high mutation rate have been given in section 5.2. It also gives an indication that genetic hill-climbing is the strategy behind the functioning of these weight optimising algorithms, which highly depend on the mutation operator to generate better solutions once the population has converged.

Since the whole group of simulations with mutation rates from 0.4 to 0.8 gave similar good results, the middle rate of 0.6 was chosen and set for the following experiments concerning crossover.

- **1-Point crossover**

A value for the mutation rate has been found experimentally $(p_m = 0.6)$, and this rate was fixed and used for all further simulations wih the crossover operators. First of all, 1-point crossover was applied, with the crossover rate p_c varying from 0.1 to 1.0 in steps of 0.1, repeating every run fifty times. A graph of the full results of these simulations is included in figure 5.3. For convenience, the average network errors after generation 50, 100 and 250 are listed in table 5.4 below.

Table 5.4 *Resulting network errors using 1-point crossover*

Gen.	\multicolumn{10}{c}{Crossover rate p_c}

Gen.	0.1	0.2	0.3	0.4	0.5	0.6	0.7	0.8	0.9	1.0
50	0.995	0.925	1.052	0.954	0.877	0.857	0.742	0.854	0.582	0.868
100	0.412	0.102	0.276	0.230	0.176	0.0709	0.151	0.0771	0.0808	0.0376
250	1.8E-1	4.1E-2	4.1E-2	4.1E-2	4.0E-2	6.4E-7	1.3E-6	3.2E-8	9.8E-7	4.8E-8

As the lines in the graphs of appendix A are quite difficult to distinguish, numbers are added for the best performing lines indicating the crossover rates of those simulations. Looking at the graph in appendix A, a few conclusions can be drawn on the results of the simulations.

First of all, it seems that the network errors tend to logarithmically approach 0, spreading out to a difference of about one order of magnitude after the first 100 generations. After that, two groups can be discerned: one group continues approaching 0 at an increased rate, while the other group slows down considerably and ultimately even remains at a constant value of about $4 \cdot 10^{-2}$. After the remaining generations, this has led to a considerable difference between the two groups of about 5 orders of magnitude. Clearly, in the latter group at least one run has become stuck at a local minimum, unable to escape within the given 250 generations. Very striking is the fact that all the members of this group are the simulations with the lower crossover rates of 0.1 up to 0.5, while the others with crossover rates of 0.6 up to 1.0 seem to have no problem whatsoever in finding many more optimal solutions. This suggests that a higher crossover rate is required for successful results. A likely reason for this is that the application of crossover guarantees that the new generation retains its diversity. When two parents are selected and inserted into the new generation without the application of crossover, it is likely that the new population loses diversity since the better chromosomes are selected more frequently, resulting in several identical chromosomes. In this process, potentially well-performing genes of other chromosomes are more likely to become lost. The algorithm then becomes solely dependant on the relatively ineffective mutation operator to introduce new genes and thus escape local minimums.

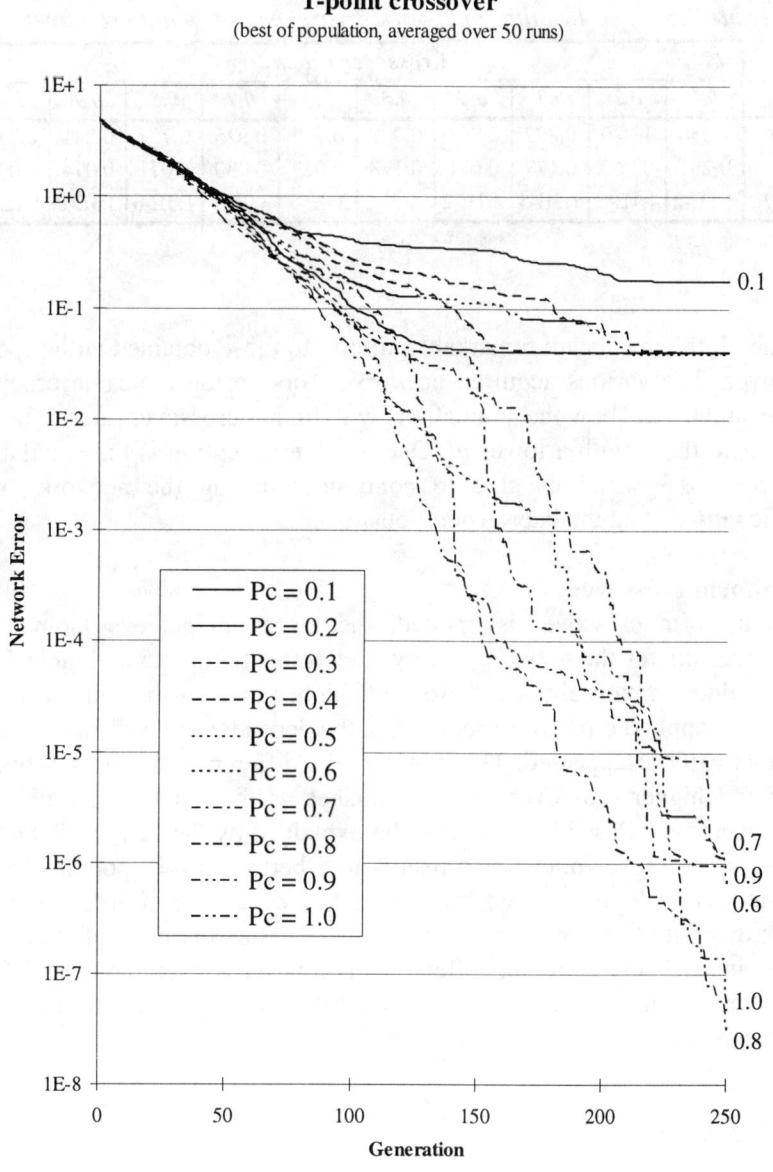

Figure 5.3   *Results using 1-point crossover (XOR problem)*

- **2-Point crossover**

The simulations described in the previous section were repeated using 2-point crossover. Again, the results are included graphically in figure 5.4, and the network errors after generations 50, 100 and 250, averaged over the 50 runs, are listed in table 5.5.

Table 5.5   *Resulting network errors using 2-point crossover*

Gen.	Crossover rate p_c									
	0.1	0.2	0.3	0.4	0.5	0.6	0.7	0.8	0.9	1.0
50	1.056	1.020	0.892	0.794	0.949	0.722	0.925	0.737	0.841	0.777
100	0.291	0.260	0.177	0.071	0.178	0.029	0.030	0.071	0.074	0.090
250	4.1E-2	4.1E-2	1.3E-5	2.1E-2	3.6E-2	2.8E-7	3.9E-7	1.5E-6	3.3E-8	1.7E-8

In general, the results are remarkably similar to those obtained with 1-point crossover. The various acquired network errors are on the same order as before, and again show the simulations with higher crossover rates to be far superior to those with a lower p_c. One notable exception is the simulation with $p_c = 0.3$ which is able to continue reducing the network error significantly during the later generations.

- **Uniform crossover**

When uniform crossover is applied, the algorithm achieves somewhat inferior results for the network error values (refer figure 5.5 and table 5.6). These values remain about a factor 100 higher than in the runs with the previously applied crossover types. Also, the dependence on crossover rates has practically disappeared. This suggests the difference in results between lower and higher crossover rates diminishes as the number of crossover points increases. Possibly, this could be explained by the fact that a higher number of crossover points also results in a better 'mixed' population, so that there is no longer a need for higher crossover rates in order to avoid loss of diversity (i.e. applying crossover sparingly at a number of crossover points instead of applying often with few crossover points). More experiments with n-point crossover operators are required to test this hypothesis.

Table 5.6   *Resulting network errors using uniform crossover*

	Crossover rate p_c									
Gen.	**0.1**	**0.2**	**0.3**	**0.4**	**0.5**	**0.6**	**0.7**	**0.8**	**0.9**	**1.0**
50	0.837	1.033	0.832	1.009	0.978	1.092	0.956	1.251	1.215	1.291
100	0.148	0.275	0.0888	0.222	0.218	0.108	0.097	0.093	0.149	0.098
250	1.9E-6	8.1E-2	7.0E-6	5.4E-2	4.1E-2	3.8E-6	3.1E-2	4.0E-2	7.1E-5	1.1E-5

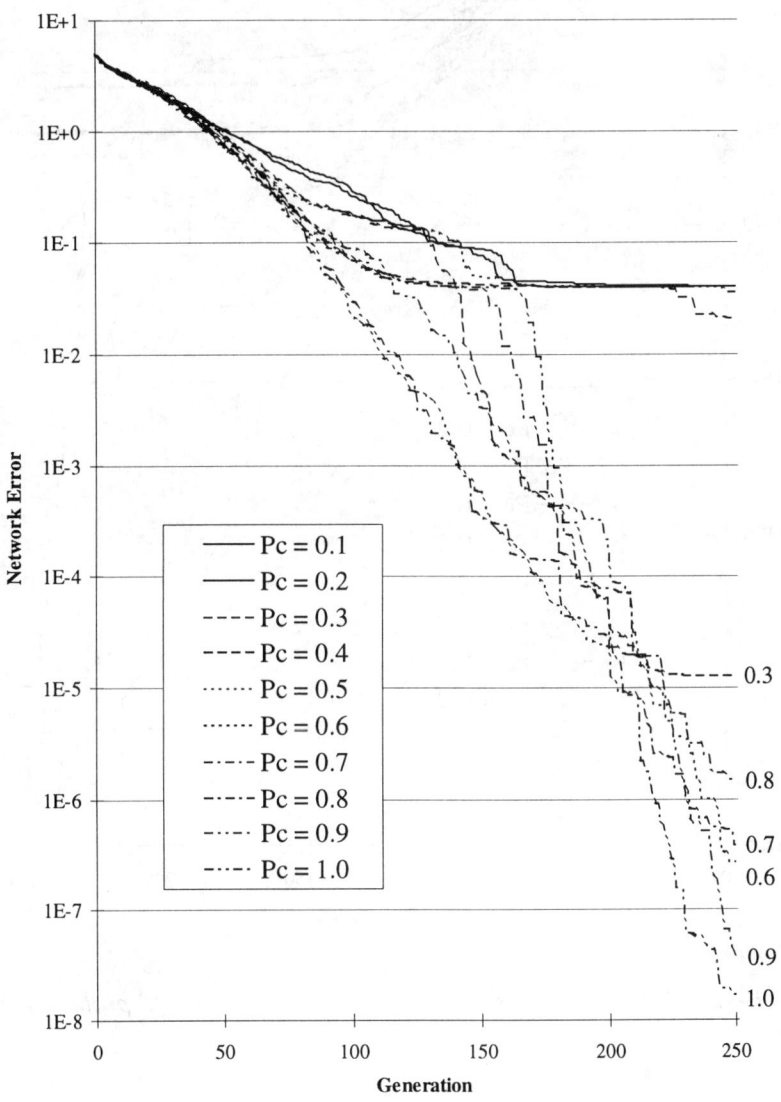

2-point crossover
(best of population, averaged over 50 runs)

Figure 5.4   *Results using 2-point crossover (XOR problem)*

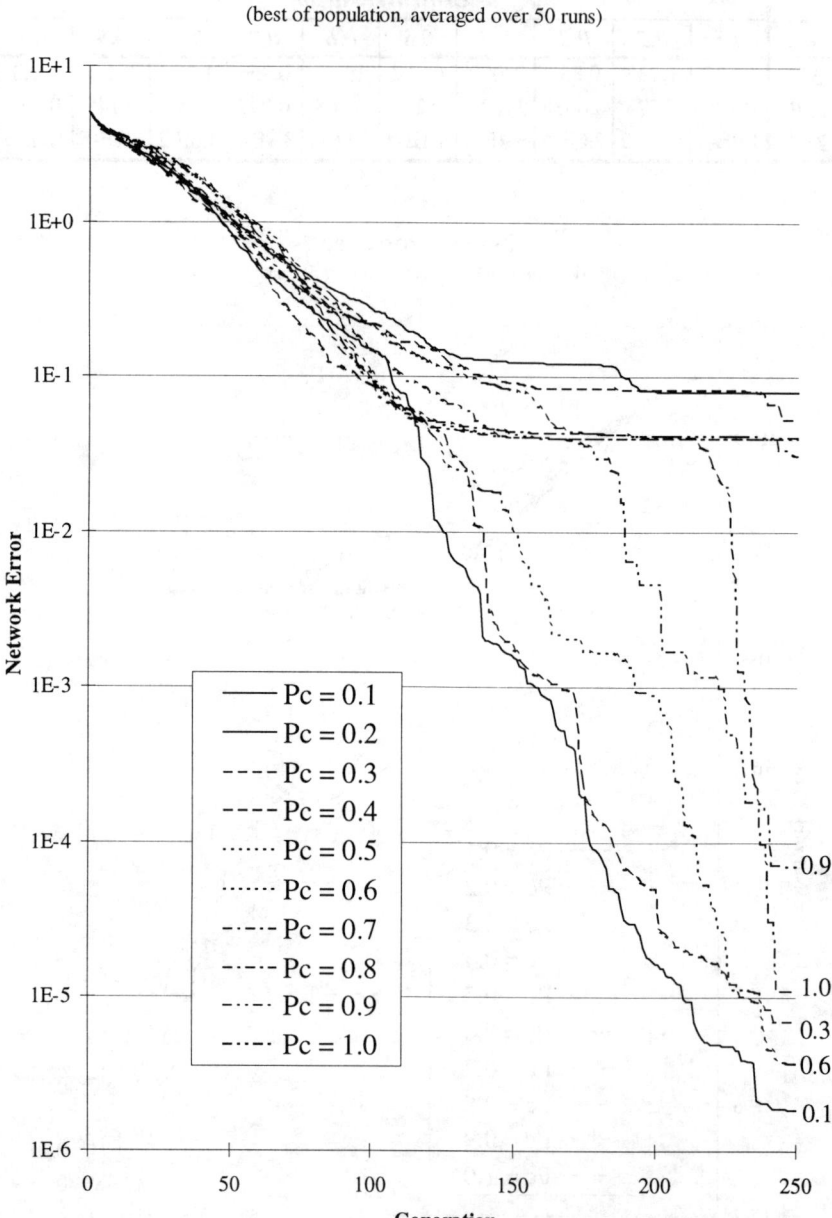

Figure 5.5   *Results using uniform crossover (XOR problem)*

• Summary

The results of the initial investigations appear to indicate that the differences between the various crossover types are not as great as was suggested by theory in the previous chapters. In approximately fifty percent of the cases, in some of the performed runs the algorithm was trapped at a local minimum. It must be realised that each line in the corresponding graphs of appendix A represents the arithmetic mean[2] of 50 different runs, which is calculated by the GA-package used for the simulations. When these results are shown in a logarithmic graph, the resulting lines favour the higher values obtained in those 50 runs. For example, when one run becomes stuck at a network error of 2 (indicating that the network coded by this chromosome misclassifies two of the training patterns), and all the other runs are continuing perfectly, obtaining very small errors of approximately $1 \cdot 10^{-10}$, then the average network error of the performed 50 runs would be 0.04, which is only two orders of magnitude away from the single value of 2, but eight orders away from the remaining 49 values of $1 \cdot 10^{-10}$. This is very likely to occur in the results obtained above, however it would take an enormous amount of work to confirm this. If the geometric mean[3] over the 50 runs was used, then the results would have given a more accurate indication of the average order of the calculated network errors. E.g., if half the runs would end up with errors of about 10^{-2} and the other half with errors of about 10^{-8}, then the geometric mean would be around 10^{-5}, whereas the arithmetic mean would still be close to 10^{-2}.

These effects of the averaging method can also explain the rather large distances which can be observed between the mean and the best value of the population in a genetic algorithm. It is to be expected that the populations lose their diversity as the algorithm progresses, and most of a population would be chasing the minimum via genetic hill-climbing, with a couple of odd members that sometimes result from a 'bad' mutation or crossover. These odd members cause the relatively high mean network error of a population.

The results obtained with 1- or 2-point crossover are, on average, better than those obtained with uniform crossover, as predicted by the Schema Theorem (see section 3.1). The differences between 1- and 2-point crossover however are less obvious, the only notable difference being that 2-point crossover also performs well with an applied rate of 0.3. It must be noted however, that the curves of figure 3.2 indicate the level of guaranteed

---

[2] The arithmetic mean is calculated as $AM = \dfrac{1}{n}\sum_{i=1}^{n} x_i = \dfrac{1}{n}\left(x_1 + x_2 + \ldots + x_n\right)$

[3] The geometric mean is calculated as $GM = \sqrt[n]{\prod_{i=1}^{n} x_i} = \sqrt[n]{\left(x_1 \cdot x_2 \cdot \ldots \cdot x_n\right)}$

non-disruption, with the possibility that the actual curve is located much higher. This is especially true when the population loses its diversity, since crossover can only disrupt schemata for which the parents' alleles do not share the same values. The equations in section 3.1 do not take this possibility of equal gene values into account and it can therefore be expected that the differences between the impact of 1- and 2-point crossover gradually disappear. This would also hold for the differences between uniform and 1- or 2-point crossover, although perhaps to a lesser degree.

Results using the NN-specific crossover operators

The experiments mentioned in section 4.3 are now considered. The value for the mutation rate ($p_m = 0.6$ per gene) was used for these experiments as in the previous section. This allowed the results for the special crossover operators to be compared with the results found in the previous section for the classic crossover operators. Again, every genetic algorithm was run for 250 generations, and repeated 50 times with identical random initial populations. For every generation the best network value (resulting from the winning chromosome of the population) was averaged over these 50 runs.

- **NN-specific 2-point crossover**

First the NN-specific 2-point crossover operator was applied, as explained in detail in section 4.3. A graph of the results is included in figure 5.6, and the usual network errors are listed in table 5.7.

Table 5.7   *Resulting network errors using NN-specific 2-point crossover*

Gen.	Crossover rate p_c									
	0.1	0.2	0.3	0.4	0.5	0.6	0.7	0.8	0.9	1.0
50	0.857	0.922	0.790	0.669	0.744	0.638	0.611	0.503	0.738	0.753
100	0.149	0.239	0.172	0.137	0.027	0.100	0.063	0.0077	0.084	0.059
250	4.0E-2	2.7E-3	8.0E-2	2.5E-6	8.1E-8	1.1E-4	4.0E-2	4.9E-11	5.5E-8	1.7E-6

Table 5.7 indicates that the crossover rate of 0.8 gave extremely good results, whereby all runs must have given very small network errors. Since this is a value averaged over 50 runs, the worst of these clearly had a network error smaller than 50 times $4.93 \cdot 10^{-11}$ (equals $2.47 \cdot 10^{-9}$), which is extremely small. Other reasonably good results were obtained using

crossover rates of 0.4, 0.5, 0.9 and 1.0, however these are not better than similar results from the normal crossover types. And there are still some crossover rates where not all runs could avoid becoming stuck in a local minimum, although in two of the five experiments, the runs appear to have made last minute escapes and produced lower error values.

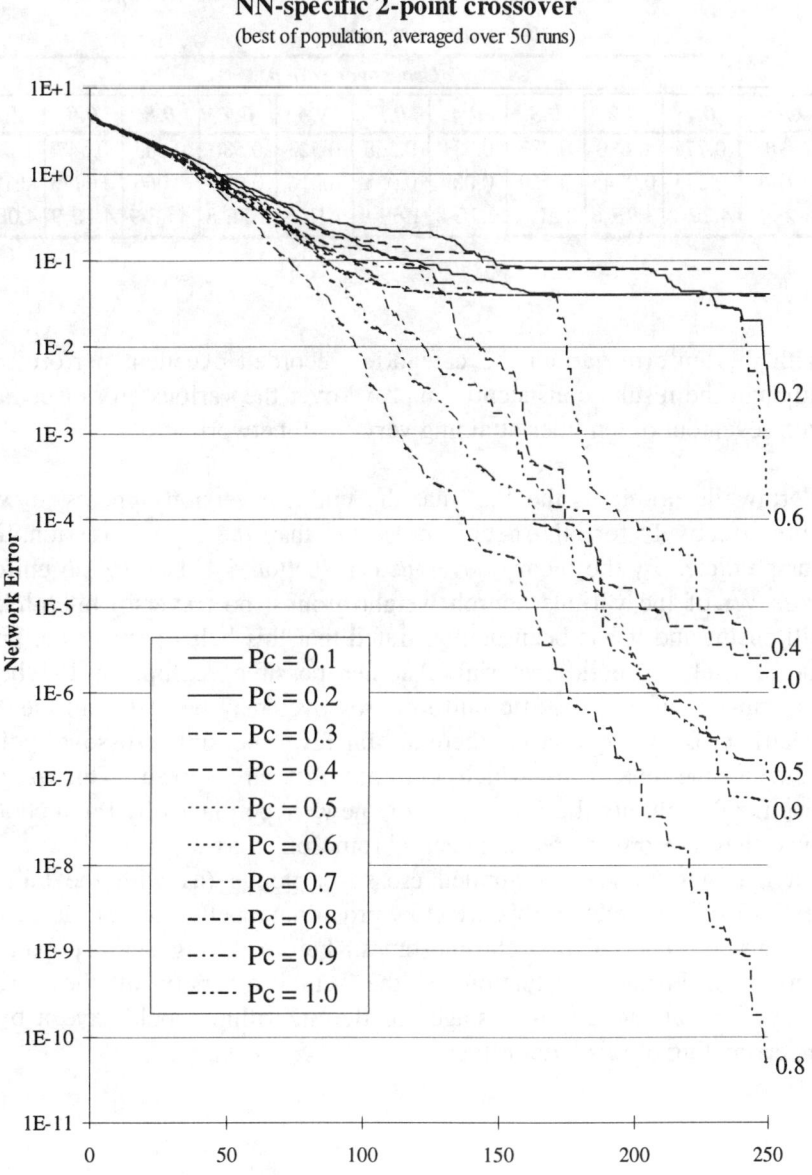

NN-specific 2-point crossover
(best of population, averaged over 50 runs)

Figure 5.6 *Results usingNN-specific 2-point crossover (XOR problem)*

- **NN-specific uniform crossover**

The NN-specific uniform crossover operator was applied next; it is also explained in detail in section 4.3. A graph of the results is included in figure 5.7, and the mean network error values are listed in table 5.8.

Table 5.8   *Resulting network errors using NN-specific uniform crossover*

Gen.	Crossover rate p_c									
	0.1	0.2	0.3	0.4	0.5	0.6	0.7	0.8	0.9	1.0
50	0.777	0.680	0.787	0.631	0.568	0.523	0.580	0.683	0.547	0.579
100	0.243	0.0245	0.169	0.082	0.055	0.016	0.075	0.066	0.0875	0.105
250	4.2E-2	1.2E-6	3.5E-2	2.7E-8	1.6E-9	1.1E-8	1.2E-8	6.6E-9	4.1E-9	4.0E-2

With the uniform variant, no categories recorded excellent performance, although the results consistently improve over the various crossover rates, with seven out of ten lines attaining very small network errors.

Worthwhile noting is the fact that the uniform version appears to work more effectively for NN-specific crossover than the 2-point version. This was predicted by the theory developed in section 4.4. Due to the uniform crossover of the various neuron weight groups, no (reverse) hitch-hiking will occur, and it has been demonstrated that this helps prevent the push-out of useful genetic material. Another possible reason for the better performance of NN-specific uniform crossover may be that with the NN-specific crossover operators, there are far fewer possible crossover points, reducing the extent to which chromosomes are mixed. This process specifically inhibits the formations of 'new' hyperplanes by this operator, since they are transferred between chromosomes as a whole. It could be that a larger number of applied crossover points (as with the uniform version) slightly reduces this effect by providing a better mix of the various neurons present in the chromosomes, before the genetic population converges. Further evaluation of the actual diversity of the various populations at the different stages of the algorithms could give a better understanding of this latter effect.

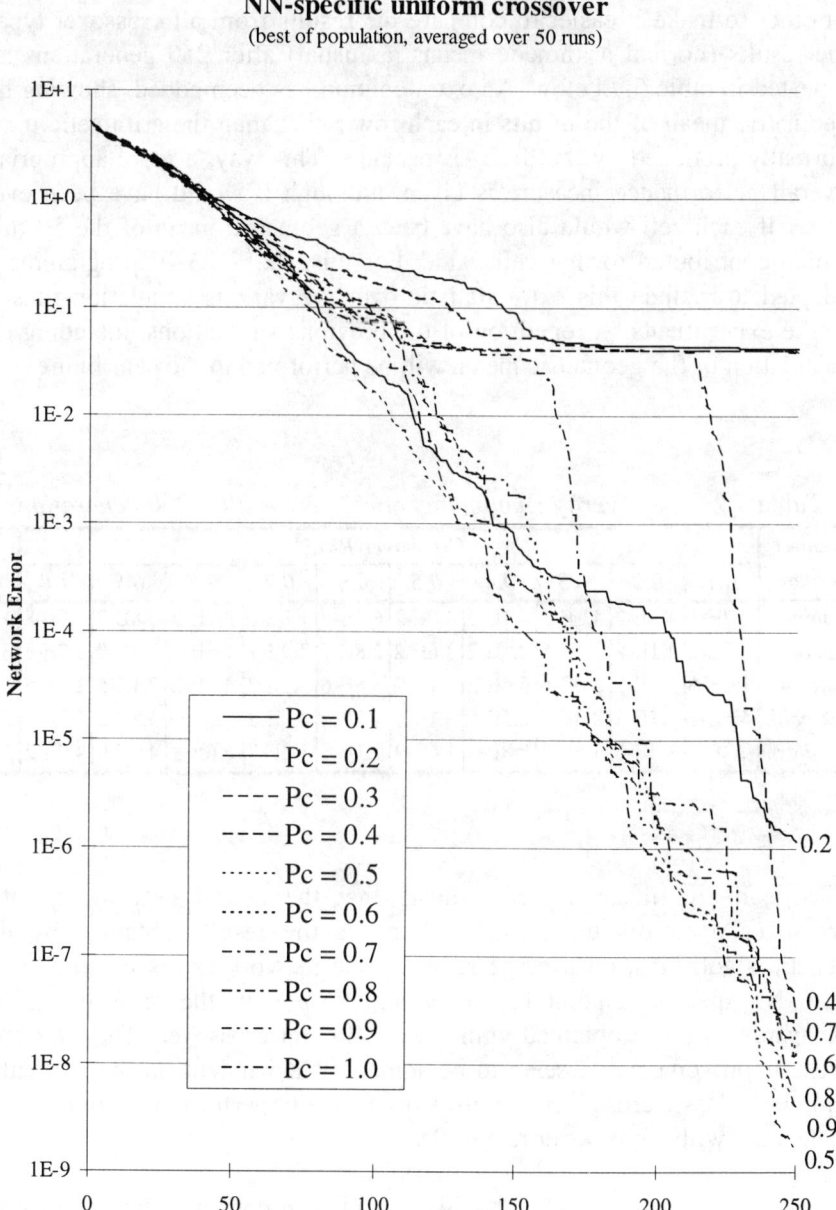

Figure 5.7   *Results using NN-specific uniform crossover (XOR problem)*

- **Summary**

In order to make it easier to compare the results from all crossover types, the results (normal arithmetic means, as usual) after 250 generations are repeated in table 5.9 below. An extra column has been added, showing the geometric mean of the results in each row rather than the arithmetic mean normally produced by the SUGAL package. This way, a more appropriate overall performance measure is given, although it would have been even better if each cell would also have been a geometric mean of the 50 runs which contributed to that cell value. For this, the SUGAL programme is adapted to include this extra statistic over the various simulation runs in future experiments. A repetition of the previous simulations, including the calculation of the geometric mean, will be performed in the near future.

Table 5.9   *Average minimum network error after 250 generations*

Crossover operator	Crossover Rate										GM
	0.1	0.2	0.3	0.4	0.5	0.6	0.7	0.8	0.9	1.0	
1-point	1.7E-1	4.1E-2	4.1E-2	4.1E-2	4.0E-2	6.4E-7	1.3E-6	3.2E-8	9.8E-7	4.8E-8	1.2E-4
2-point	4.1E-2	4.1E-2	1.3E-5	2.1E-2	3.6E-2	2.8E-7	3.9E-7	1.5E-6	3.3E-8	1.7E-8	3.3E-5
uniform	1.9E-6	8.1E-2	7.0E-6	5.4E-2	4.1E-2	3.8E-6	3.1E-2	4.0E-2	7.1E-5	1.1E-5	6.3E-4
NN-2-point	4.0E-2	2.7E-3	8.0E-2	2.5E-6	8.1E-8	1.1E-4	4.0E-2	4.9E-11	5.5E-8	1.7E-6	2.3E-5
NN-uniform	4.2E-2	1.2E-6	3.5E-2	2.8E-8	1.6E-9	1.1E-8	1.2E-8	6.6E-9	4.0E-9	4.0E-2	1.3E-6

The geometric mean values indicate that the neural network specific crossover operators unmistakably improve the results obtained by the genetic algorithms, on average reducing the network errors between 32% with NN-specific 2-point crossover and 96% with the uniform variant compared to those obtained with classic 2-point crossover. The extent of these improvements do seem to be somewhat dependent on the particular run, with classic crossover operators occasionally performing better, e.g. as is the case with a crossover rate of 0.9.

However, the above figures should be read with consideration to possible limitations, some of which have already been discussed in earlier stages in this book:

- The use of the arithmetic mean can severely obscure the real performance of the genetic algorithm, rendering the impact of a single poor result far graver than what seems to be 'fair'. Therefore, some results may not give an accurate indication as to what average order is usually obtained for the network error.

- The results are taken from 50 individual runs, due to the time restrictions of the computational requirements. Although 50 is a reasonably high number compared to other studies (many researchers of genetic algorithms base their conclusions on as little as 10 runs), it can still be considered as low from a statistical point of view. Again, this allows a single 'unlucky' poor result to significantly colour the results. For example, this could happen when two batches of runs are compared against each other, of which one batch indeed comprises one of these unlucky results, where the other batch of runs does not. Then, the latter batch would seem to perform a great deal more effectively, even though the overall performances of the two batches were similar, apart from the single unlucky event.

5.2 The 'iris flower' problem

The iris flower data set consists of a training set of 75 patterns. A single pattern contains four real-valued input values on [0,1] and three binary output values. The class of a pattern is determined by the output which has a value of one; the other two outputs are always zero. The input data represent four attributes of the iris flowers according to which they are categorised into three classes. The neural network proposed for classifying this data was a fully connected feed-forward neural network, with four input neurons, four hidden neurons and three output neurons. Including the standard neuron thresholds, the genetic algorithm requires chromosomes with 35 genes.

The normal GA-parameters are set as described in section 4.2. The mutation rate is set to $p_m = 0.6$ as with the continuous XOR problem in the previous section. Since the results with the XOR problem indicated the best results are obtained using high crossover rates, simulations are completed with this crossover rate set to $p_c = 0.6$, 0.8 and 1.0 respectively. This choice of crossover rates limits the number of simulations to be performed by the genetic algorithm, however is expected to provide useful insight into the GA's performance for this problem. As with the continuous XOR problem, the genetic algorithm is run for 250 generations, since convergence is usually obtained within this limit, which means that all test patterns are usually classified correctly.

Simulation results

Simulations were performed with the three standard crossover types (1-point, 2-point and uniform) and the two NN-specific crossover types introduced in chapter 4 (NN-specific 2-point and NN-specific uniform).

Every setting was tested 25 times, each time with different random initialisations, and the results were averaged (before starting the simulations, SUGAL was modified so that as well as the arithmetic mean the geometric mean was available). Full graphic results of these simulations are included in figures 5.8 to 5.10.

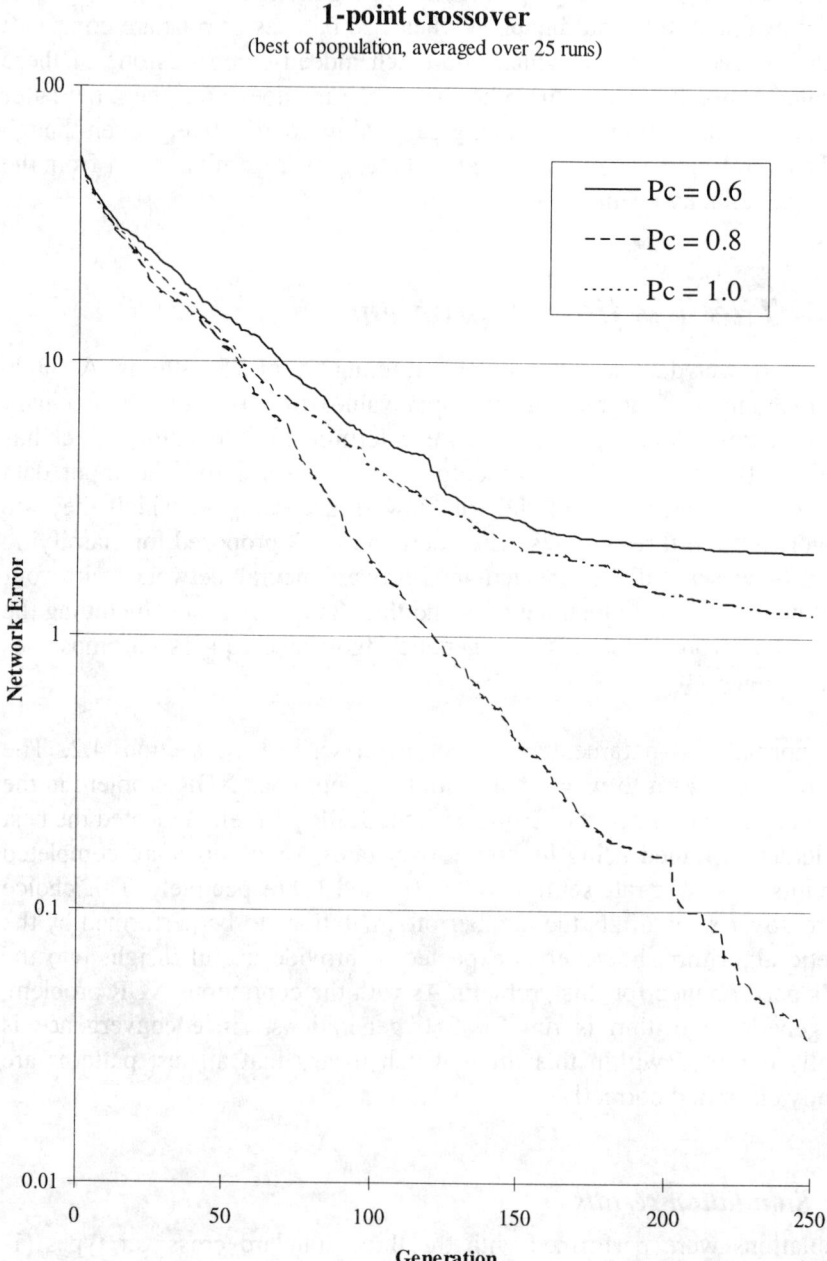

Figure 5.8   *Results using 1-point crossover (iris problem)*

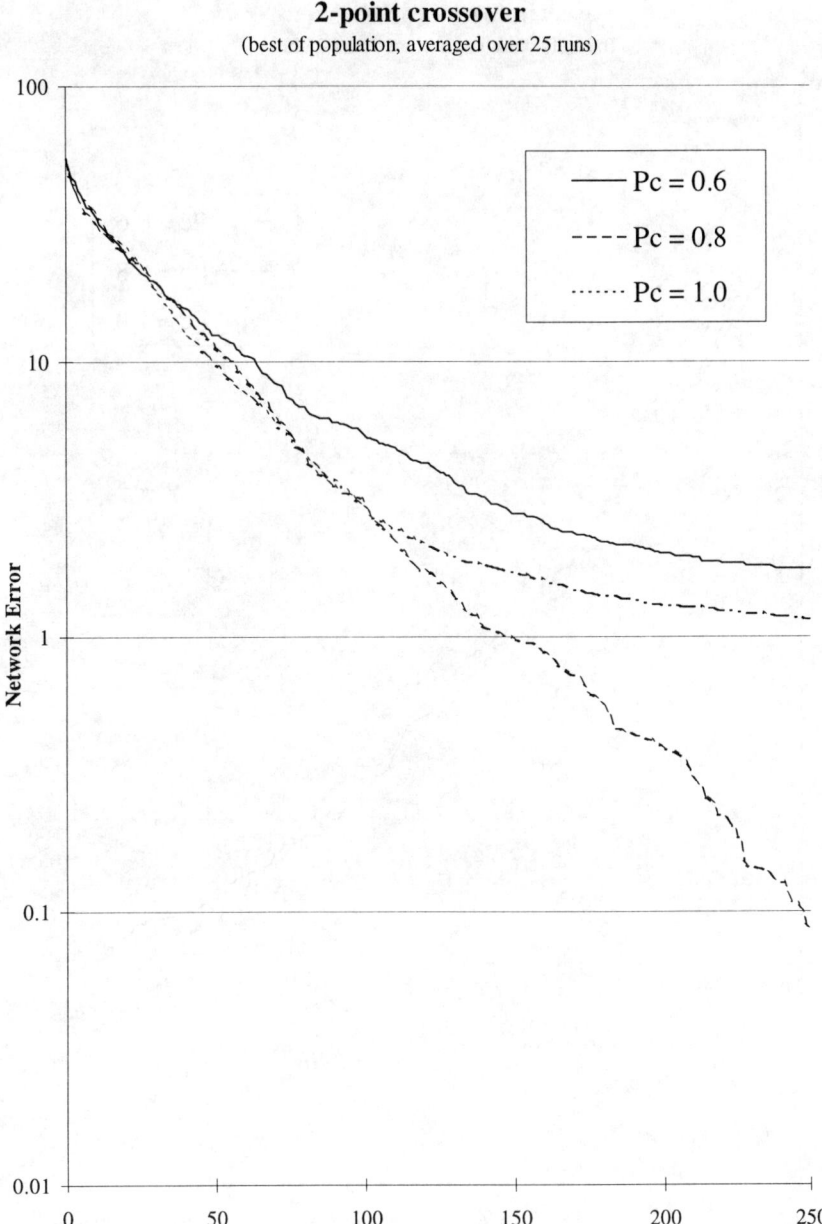

2-point crossover
(best of population, averaged over 25 runs)

Pc = 0.6
Pc = 0.8
Pc = 1.0

Network Error

Generation

Figure 5.9 *Results using 2-point crossover (iris problem)*

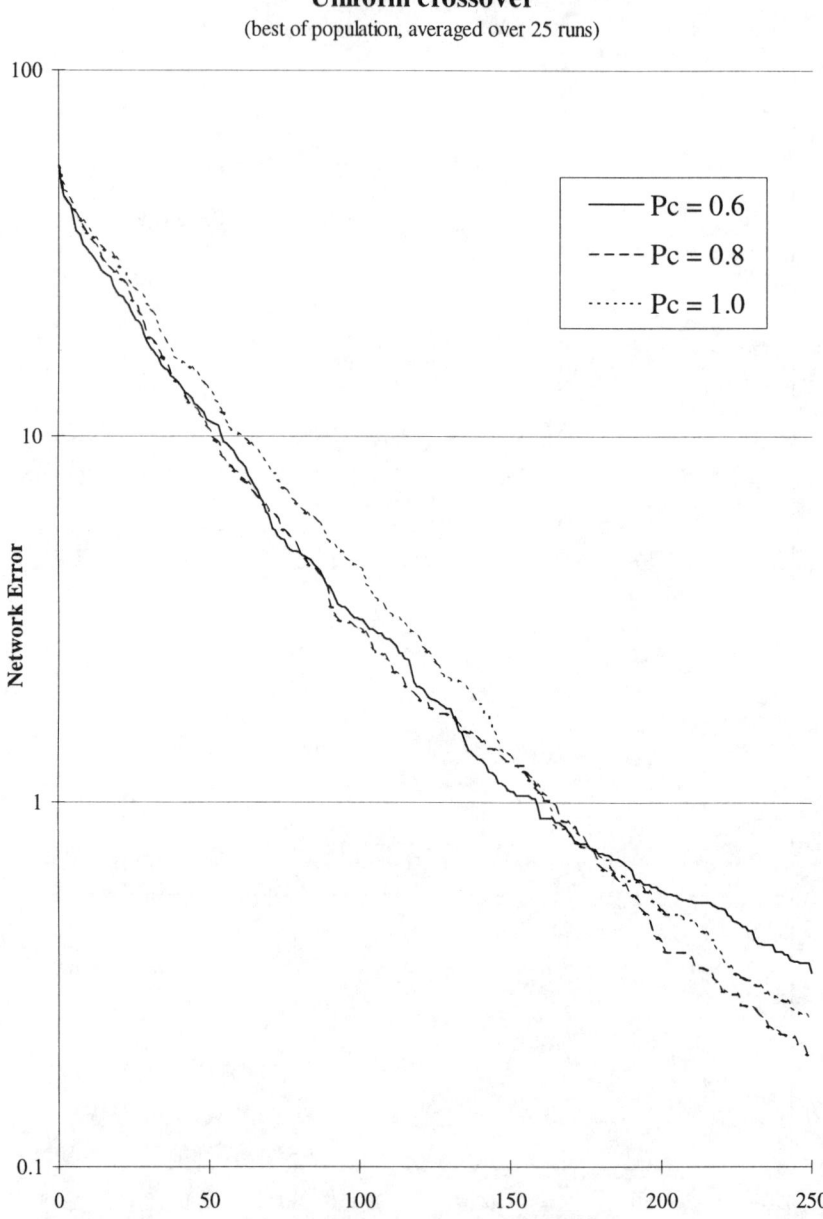

Uniform crossover

(best of population, averaged over 25 runs)

Figure 5.10   *Results using uniform crossover (iris problem)*

In table 5.10, some results for 1-point crossover are listed, both for the arithmetic and the geometric mean. Table 5.11 and table 5.12 contain similar information for 2-point and uniform crossovers.

Table 5.10   *Resulting network errors using the
1-point crossover operator*

	Average of the runs			Geometric mean of the runs		
Generation	$p_c = 0.6$	$p_c = 0.8$	$p_c = 1.0$	$p_c = 0.6$	$p_c = 0.8$	$p_c = 1.0$
100	5.30	1.87	4.13	2.29	1.40	2.07
250	2.05	3.23E-2	1.22	1.05E-2	5.12E-3	1.88E-2

Table 5.11   *Resulting network errors using the
2-point crossover operator*

	Average of the runs			Geometric mean of the runs		
Generation	$p_c = 0.6$	$p_c = 0.8$	$p_c = 1.0$	$p_c = 0.6$	$p_c = 0.8$	$p_c = 1.0$
100	5.46	2.99	3.00	3.11	2.38	1.91
250	1.77	8.44E-2	1.17	5.36E-2	1.65E-2	2.41E-2

Table 5.12   *Resulting network errors using the
uniform crossover operator*

	Average of the runs			Geometric mean of the runs		
Generation	$p_c = 0.6$	$p_c = 0.8$	$p_c = 1.0$	$p_c = 0.6$	$p_c = 0.8$	$p_c = 1.0$
100	3.17	2.99	4.43	2.14	1.96	3.44
250	0.343	0.204	0.255	6.28E-2	4.25E-2	4.25E-2

This data indicate that one or more runs commonly fails to classify all input patterns correctly, resulting in high average network errors for the best of each population. The values for the geometric mean aid in interpreting these average values, since the average order of magnitude of the results is about 10^{-2}. This is obviously low enough to ensure a 100% correct classification rate. Both the arithmetic and the geometric mean indicate that the resulting network errors are almost always lowest for the crossover rate of $p_c = 0.8$. Furthermore, the geometric mean values show that 1-point and 2-point crossover perform somewhat better than uniform crossover, as predicted by the theory there does not appear to be a great deal of difference between the crossover rates of 0.6, 0.8 and 1.0 for any of the crossover operators.

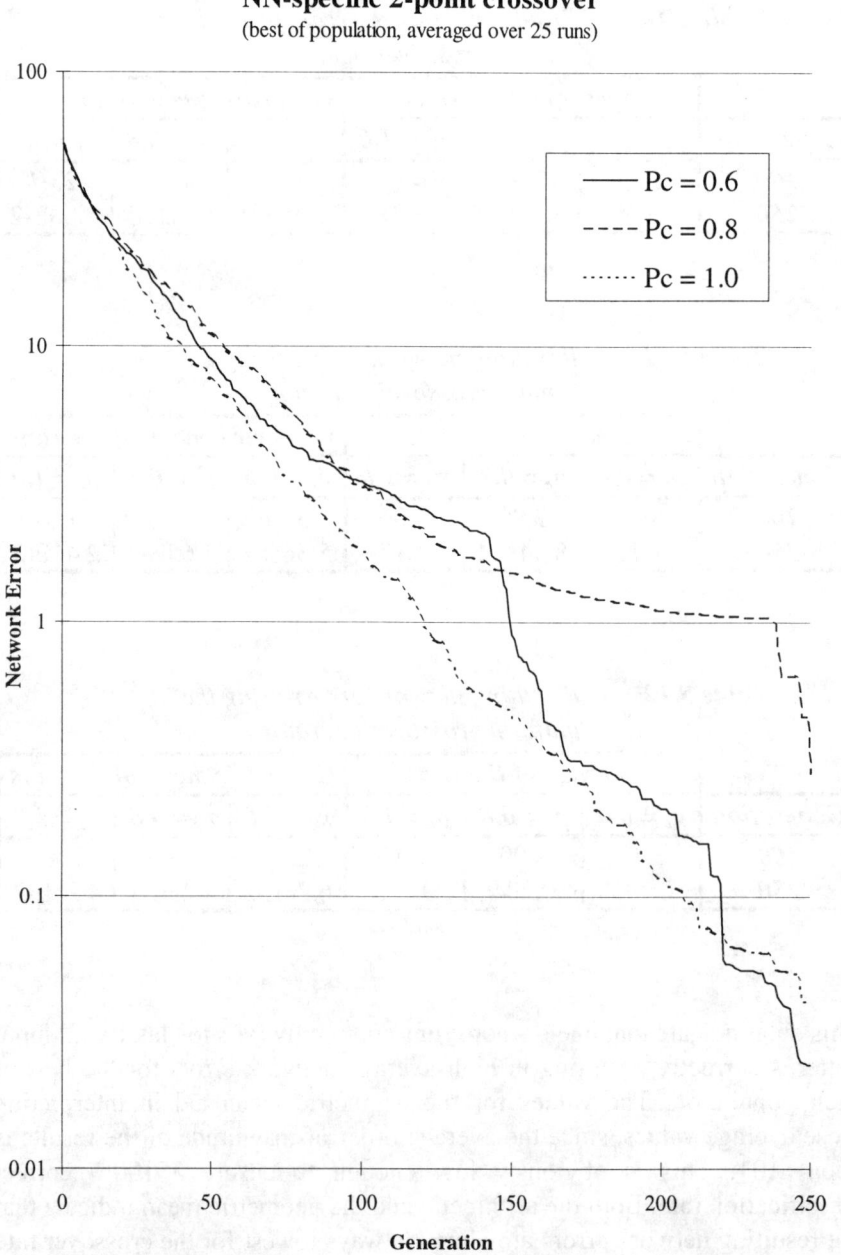

NN-specific 2-point crossover
(best of population, averaged over 25 runs)

Figure 5.11   *Results using NN-specific 2-point crossover (iris problem)*

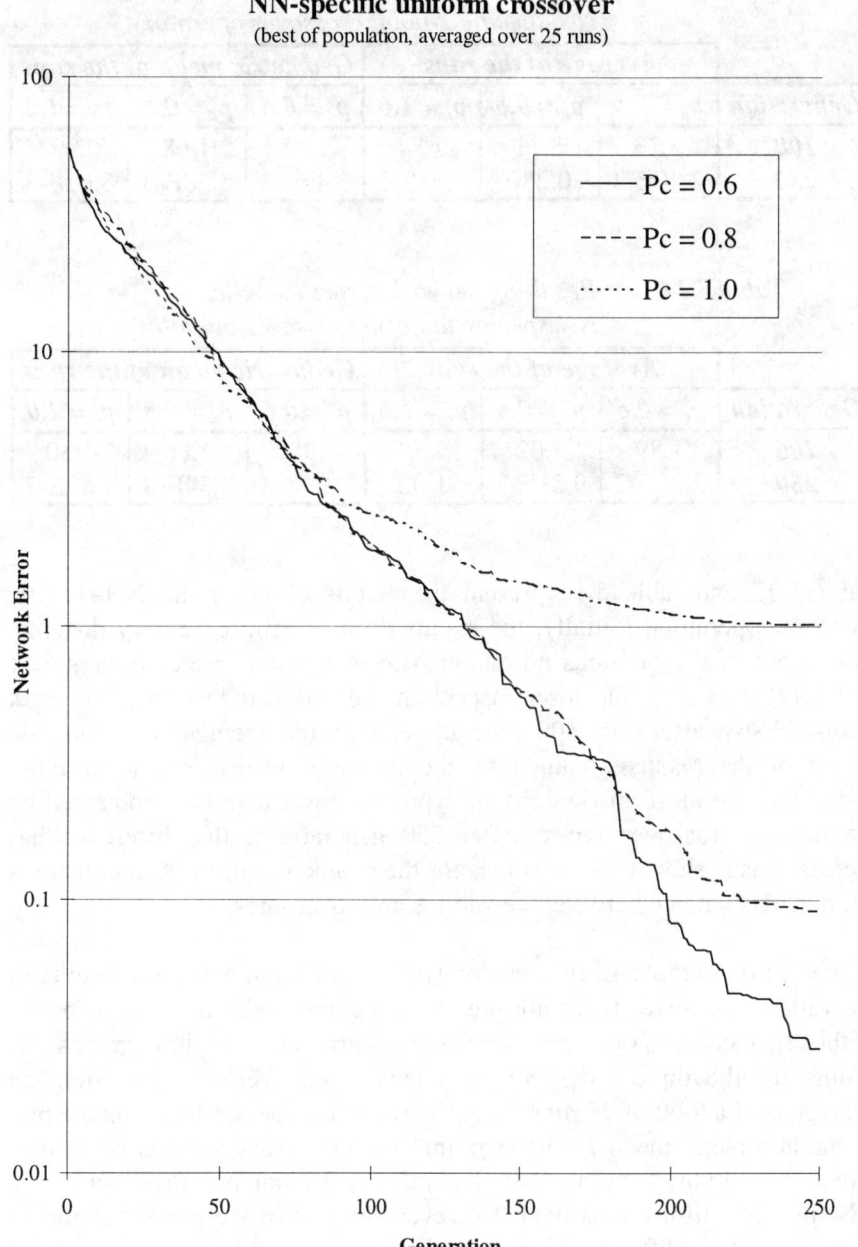

Figure 5.12   *Results using NN-specific uniform crossover (iris problem)*

Table 5.13 *Resulting network errors using the NN-specific 2-point crossover operator*

Generation	Average of the runs			Geometric mean of the runs		
	$p_c = 0.6$	$p_c = 0.8$	$p_c = 1.0$	$p_c = 0.6$	$p_c = 0.8$	$p_c = 1.0$
100	3.23	3.11	1.84	1.63	1.68	0.993
250	2.40E-2	0.280	4.08E-2	3.47E-3	5.58E-3	3.62E-3

Table 5.14 *Resulting network errors using the NN-specific uniform crossover operator*

Generation	Average of the runs			Geometric mean of the runs		
	$p_c = 0.6$	$p_c = 0.8$	$p_c = 1.0$	$p_c = 0.6$	$p_c = 0.8$	$p_c = 1.0$
100	1.89	2.02	2.58	0.989	1.06	1.30
250	2.89E-2	9.21E-2	1.02	2.96E-3	2.34E-3	1.69E-3

Table 5.13 and table 5.14 present the results of using the NN-specific crossover operators. Initially, the results do not seem to be very different from those of the previous normal crossover operators (refer figures 5.11 and 5.12), however on closer inspection there is a reduction in network errors. Firstly, after only 100 generations, both the average and geometric means of the results obtained by the two NN-specific crossover types (especially the uniform version) are typically lower than those obtained by the normal crossover types. After 250 generations, the difference has increased as is shown by the values for the geometric mean. Again, there is not much difference between the various crossover rates.

In the last two graphs of this section (figures 5.13 and 5.14), the results of the various crossover types are presented together, with one graph for the arithmetic mean and one graph for the geometric mean. In these graphs, the results for the three crossover rates have been averaged, providing an average over a total of 75 runs for each crossover type. Considering the plot of the arithmetic means, it appears that uniform crossover has performed rather well, outperforming both 1-point and 2-point crossover and even NN-specific uniform crossover. However, the plot of the geometric means presents quite a different picture, with uniform crossover performing the worst of all. This poor performance is undoubtedly caused by the fact that with the other crossover types one or more unlucky runs became stuck at a local minimum with a reasonably high network error. This plot of the geometric means therefore gives a better impression of the actual performance of the various crossover types, without any results being overshadowed by a single unlucky run. It also indicates that the results are in line with the presented theory, with uniform crossover performing the worst, and the NN-specific crossover types producing the best results. Again, NN-specific uniform crossover performs slightly better than NN-specific 2-point crossover, which again is probably due to the fact that (reverse) hitch-hiking is avoided and that a better mix of the available, well performing hyperplanes is made.

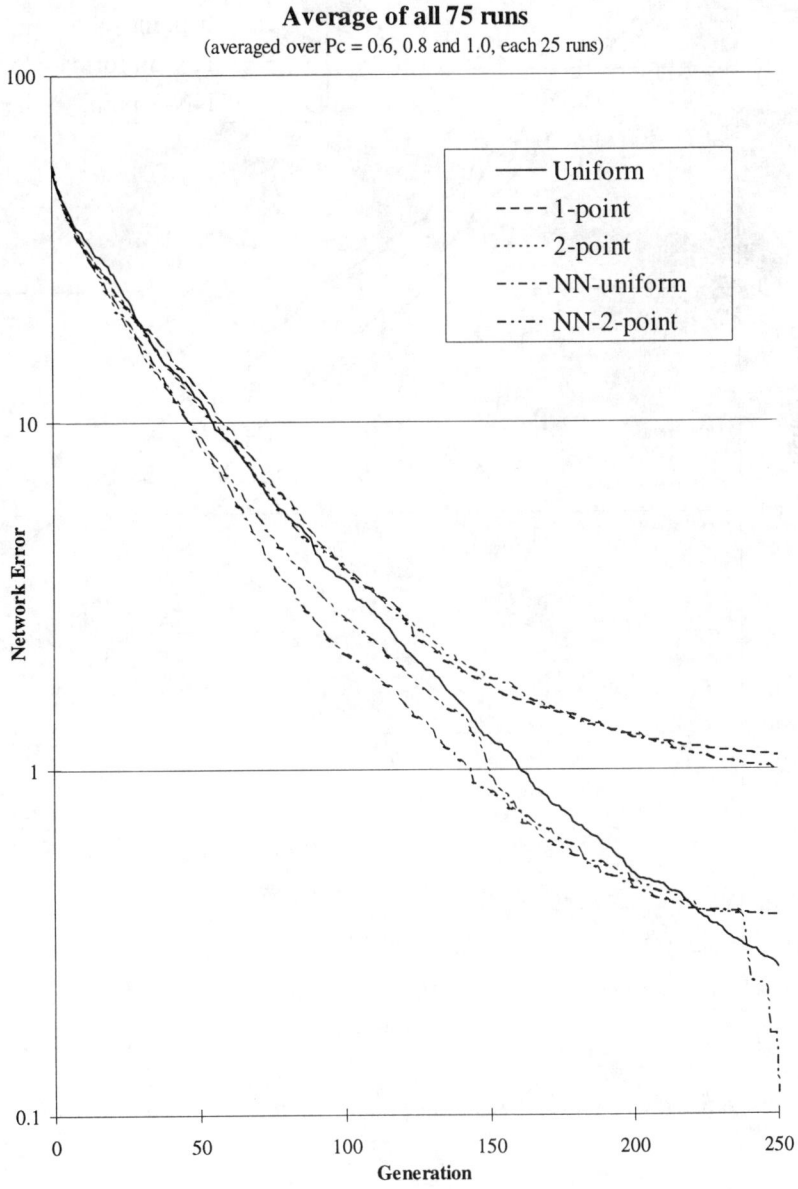

Figure 5.13   *Average results (arithmetic mean) for the iris problem*

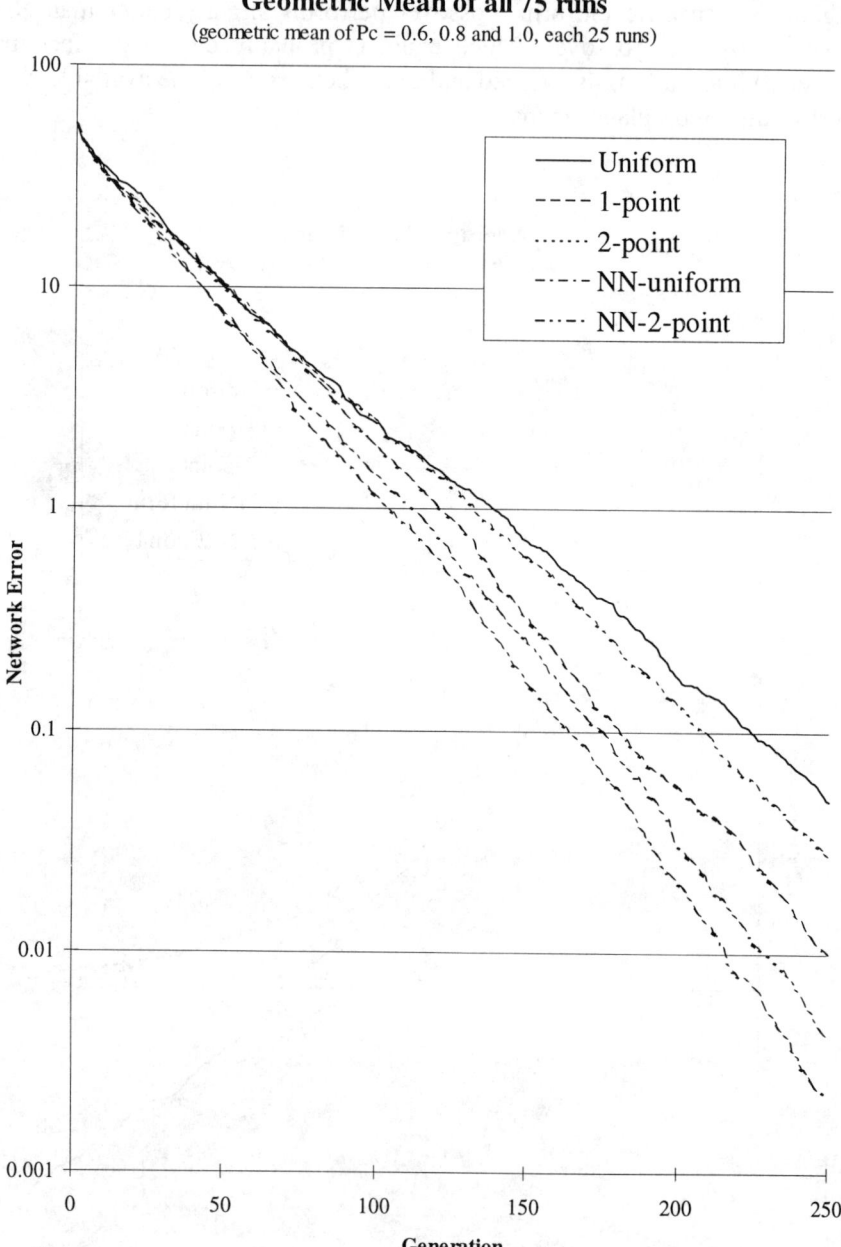

Figure 5.14   *Average results (geometric mean) for the iris problem*

5.3 The 'dice' problem

The dice problem is a self-made problem. It requires a neural network to recognise the dots on a dice, aligned in a three by three pattern, as a number ranging from one to six. This must be performed regardless of the position of the dice, e.g. the dot pattern can be rotated. Figure 5.15 demonstrates all possible dot patterns.

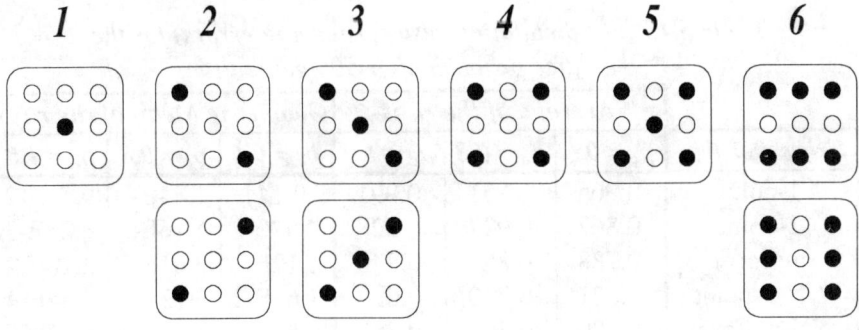

Figure 5.15   *All possible dot input patterns for the dice problem*

The input data consists of nine input values, which can be either the value +1 (dot) or −1 (no dot). These values are taken directly from the pattern, row by row starting from the top, from left to right. The output data consists of six binary values, classifying the input into one of six classes: a '1' signifies the present input pattern is a member of this class, a '0' means it is not. The six output classes are the possible dice numbers of one to six. The neural network used to classify the data was a fully connected feed-forward neural network, with nine input neurons, six hidden neurons and six output neurons. Including the standard neuron thresholds, the genetic algorithm requires chromosomes with 102 genes.

The normal GA-parameters are set as described in section 4.2. The mutation rate is again set to $p_m = 0.6$, and simulations are performed with this crossover rate set to $p_c = 0.6$, 0.8 and 1.0 respectively. The genetic algorithm is run for 500 generations.

Simulation results

Every parameter setting is run 25 times, each time with different random initialisations. The network errors of the best chromosome of each generation are accumulated. Figures 5.16 and 5.17 show the average and geometric mean of these network errors over all three settings. Table 5.15 details the results, obtained by the various crossover operators after the 500 generations, per setting for the crossover rate.

Table 5.15   *Simulation results (network errors) for the*
dice problem after 500 generations

	Average of the runs			Geometric Mean of the runs		
Crossover type	$p_c = 0.6$	$p_c = 0.8$	$p_c = 1.0$	$p_c = 0.6$	$p_c = 0.8$	$p_c = 1.0$
1-point	0.965	0.851	0.891	0.144	1.44E-2	9.58E-2
2-point	0.862	0.927	0.828	4.57E-2	5.16E-3	8.28E-3
uniform	0.788	0.880	0.840	1.12E-2	4.01E-3	2.10E-2
NN-2-point	0.821	0.720	0.693	1.65E-2	3.12E-3	8.54E-4
NN-uniform	0.480	0.364	0.360	6.60E-4	1.79E-5	5.67E-6

It appears that the average values are reasonably high, indicating that in each batch of 25 runs, at least a couple of runs did not reach a network error close to zero, but stayed in a local minimum where not all input patterns were correctly classified. The geometric mean values do indicate that a correct solution has indeed been found in many other runs, obtaining very small network errors. As distinct from the previous problem of the iris flower classification, with this problem there is a noticeable difference between the results from the different crossover rates: $p_c = 0.8$ performs best for the normal crossover types, and the performance of the NN-specific crossover types strongly improves as the crossover rate increases.

From both the average and geometric mean values of table 5.15, it is clear that the NN-specific operators significantly outperform the normal crossover operators. This can also be readily seen from figures 5.16 and 5.17. Once again, it is NN-specific uniform crossover that obtains the best results, as predicted by theory.

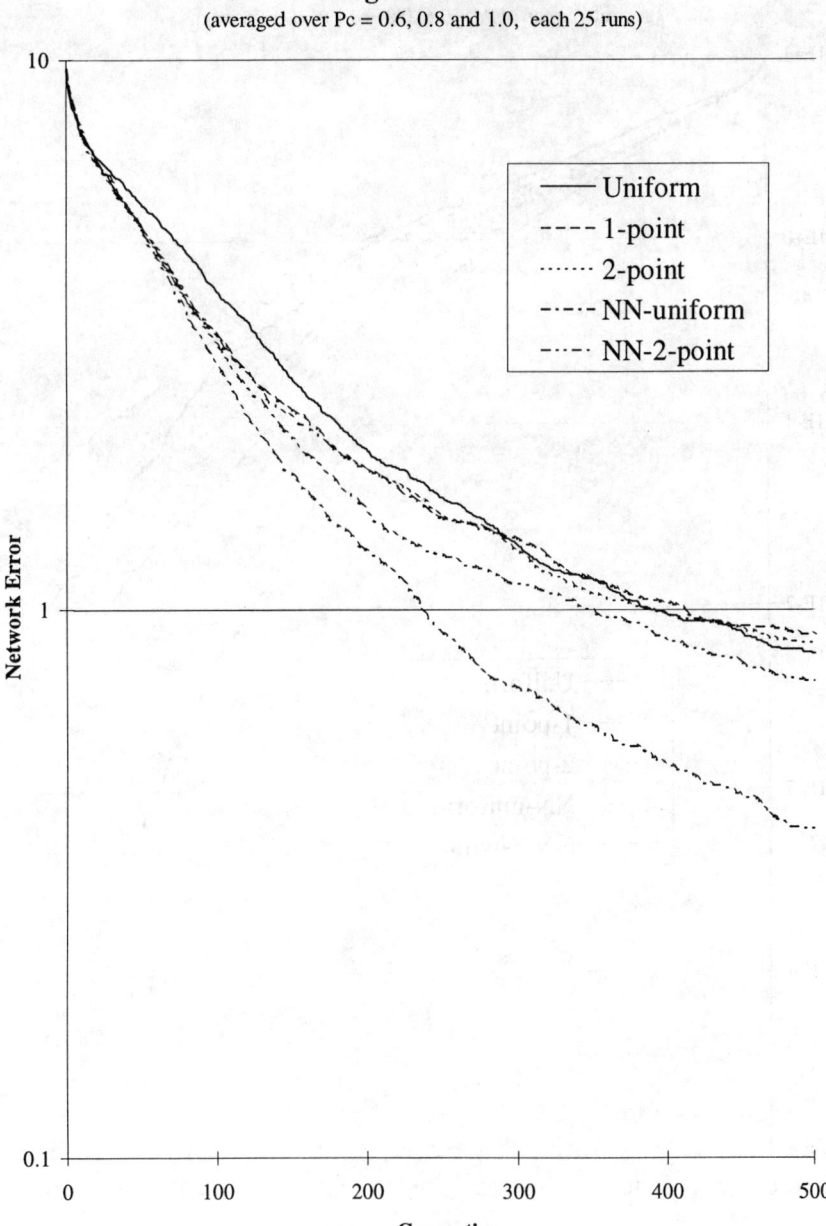

Figure 5.16 *Average results (arithmetic mean) for the dice problem*

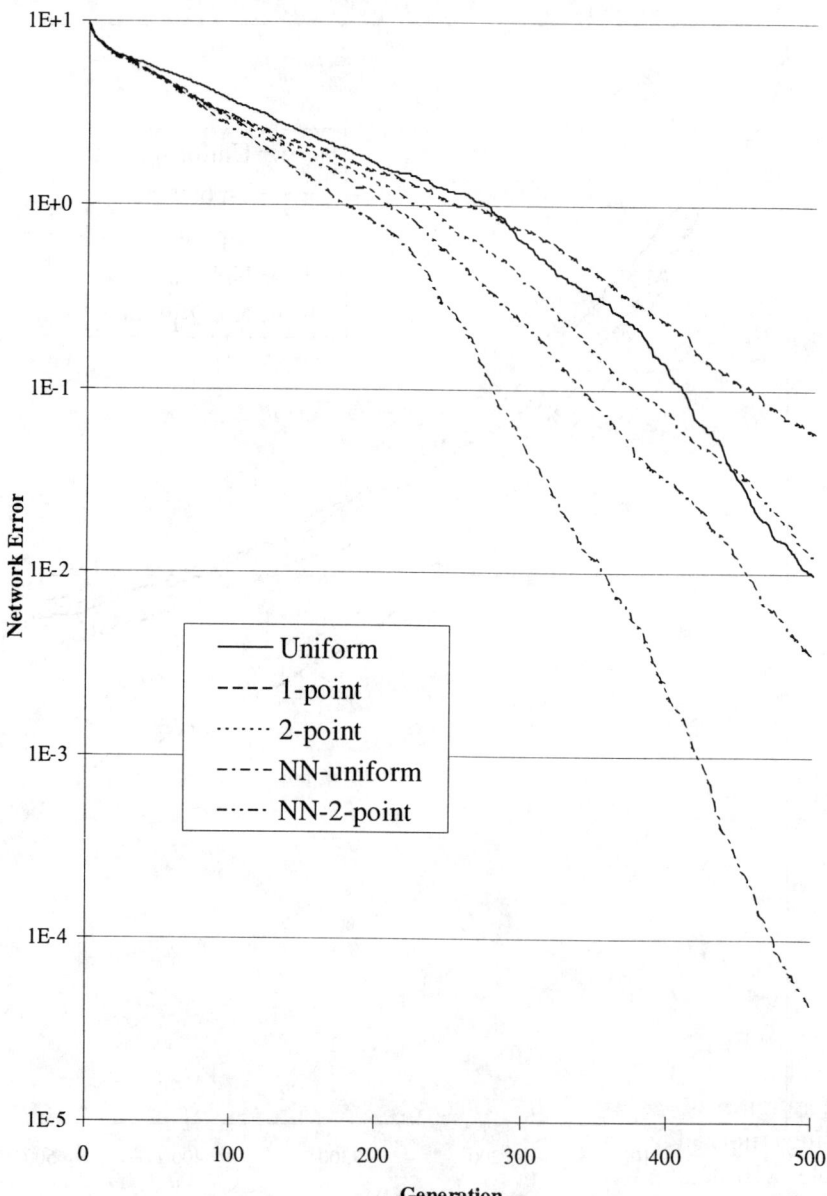

Figure 5.17   *Average results (arithmetic mean) for the dice problem*

5.4   The 'heart disease' problem

The heart disease problem was the first real world problem to be solved by the genetic algorithms developed in this book. It involves the detection of the presence of heart disease, based on basic patient information[4]. The aim is to use a trained neural network for the diagnosis of potential patients. The original database contained 303 instances, but six of these contained incomplete data and have therefore been discarded. Of the resulting 297 vectors, only the first 100 have actually been used in the experiments here, due to time restrictions on the simulations.

Each vector contains thirteen real-valued components, and one output value. All inputs have been scaled into the same range from −10 to +10. The output value refers to the presence of heart disease in the patient, and is an integer valued from 0 (no presence) to 4 (heavy presence). According to the source of the medical database, previous experiments have all been aiming to distinguish no presence (value 0) from presence (values 1, 2, 3 and 4) of heart disease. This same procedure has been adopted here, resulting in 57 targets of zero, and 43 targets of one (the original output values of 1 to 4).

The neural network used to classify the data was a fully connected feed-forward neural network, with thirteen input neurons, ten hidden neurons and one output neuron. Including the standard neuron thresholds, the genetic algorithm requires chromosomes with 151 genes. The normal GA-parameters were set as described in section 4.2. The mutation rate was set to $p_m = 0.6$, as before, and simulations were performed with the crossover rate set to $p_c = 0.6$, 0.8 and 1.0 respectively. The genetic algorithm was run for 500 generations.

Simulation results

Every setting was run 25 times, each time with different random initialisations. The network errors of the best chromosome of each generation were accumulated, averaged over the experiments of the three settings (normal average) and plotted. This graph is included as figure 5.18. Table 5.16 details the results obtained by the various crossover operators after the 500 generations, per setting for the crossover rate.

---

[4] The heart disease database, which has been used here as the training set, has been collected by Robert Detrano, M.D., Ph.D., from the V.A. Medical Center, Long Beach and the Cleveland Clinic Foundation.

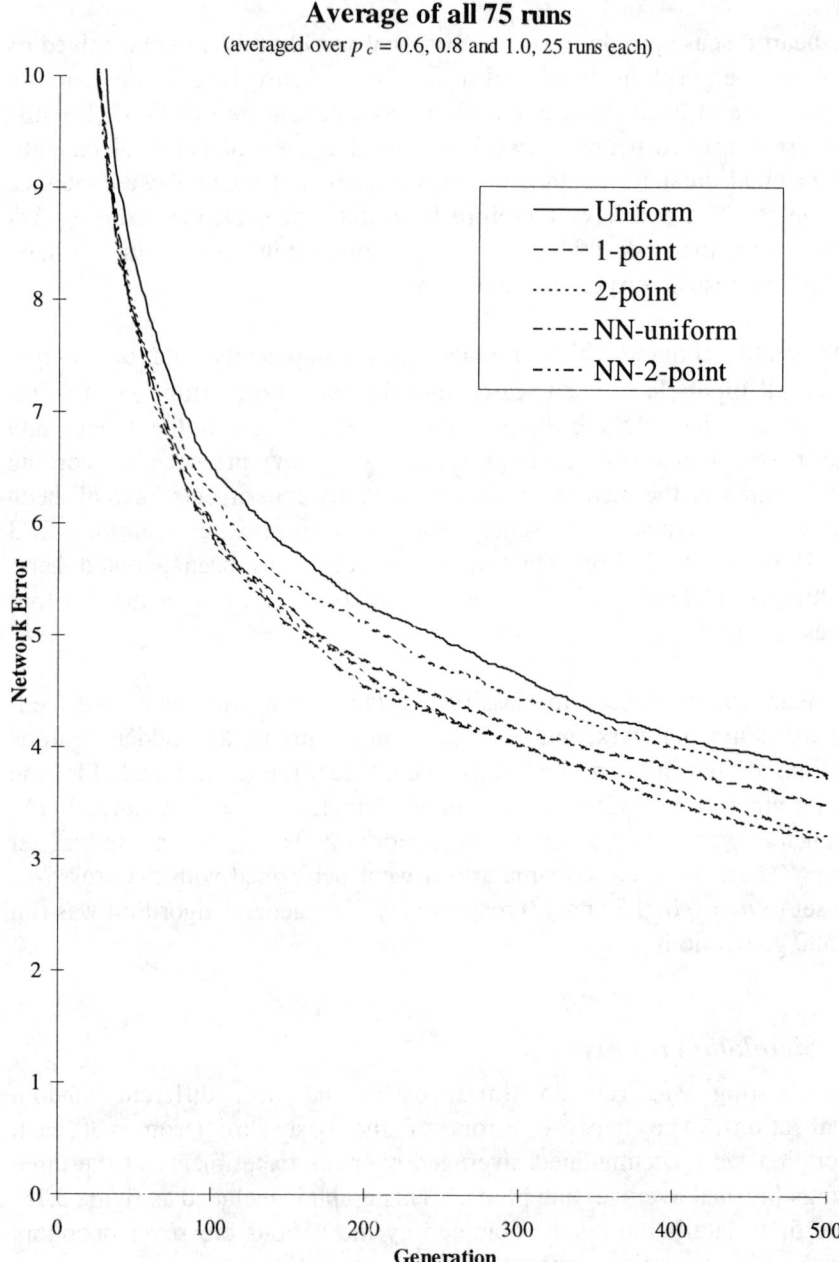

Figure 5.18   *Average results (arithmetic mean) for the heart problem*

Table 5.16   *Simulation results (network error) for the heart disease problem after 500 generations*

Crossover type	Average of the runs			Geometric Mean of the runs		
	$p_c = 0.6$	$p_c = 0.8$	$p_c = 1.0$	$p_c = 0.6$	$p_c = 0.8$	$p_c = 1.0$
1-point	3.616	3.683	3.279	3.501	3.581	3.133
2-point	4.116	3.750	3.404	4.028	3.582	3.213
uniform	4.077	3.812	3.492	3.950	3.613	3.307
NN-2-point	3.555	3.279	2.907	3.345	3.089	2.702
NN-uniform	3.276	3.205	3.129	3.147	2.950	2.902

The resulting network errors indicate that many of the runs did not reach a perfect classification of all the input vectors. In contrast to the previous problem, the geometric mean values are not reduced below values of around three to four. And although the graph (refer **figure** 5.18) indicates that the genetic algorithms continue to reduce the network error, perfect solutions are not likely to be found using the chosen limited training regime. In fact, the lowest network errors to be found by each crossover type in all runs, were 1.001 for 1-point crossover, 0.962 for 2-point crossover, 1.000 for uniform crossover, 0.891 for NN-specific uniform crossover and finally 0.998 for NN-specific 2-point crossover. These values are almost equal, but almost certainly still not low enough to guarantee a 100 % classification. Based on table 5.16, it can be estimated that, after 500 generations, on average three training vectors remain misclassified, which equals a correct classification rate of 97.5 %.

The simulation error results improve as the crossover rate increases from 0.6 to 1.0. This also occurred in the dice problem when using the NN-specific crossover types, but here it applies to all types. The 1-point crossover performs best for the classic versions. For the NN-specific types, the uniform version performs better for $p_c = 0.6$, equal results are obtained for $p_c = 0.8$, and the 2-point version performs better for the highest crossover rate. This means that for the first time uniform NN-specific crossover does not always give the best results. It is clear that the NN-specific operators outperform the normal crossover operators, although the difference is not very great.

5.5   The 'ship' problem

The last and biggest problem in this series concerns the classification of ships. It is a real life problem, for which the database was made available by DSTO[5] of Australia. The original database was reduced to retain the first ten vectors for each output class have been used to limit the computing times. Since there are twelve possible output classes, this resulted in a total of 120 input vectors.

Each vector contains seventeen real-valued input values, and twelve output values representing twelve categories of ships. The input values refer to the shape description of ships. Overall, seventeen real-valued inputs are used in each vector, the resulting values being scaled into the same range (-10 to $+10$) as before.

The neural network used to classify the data was a fully connected feed-forward neural network, with seventeen input neurons, twelve hidden neurons and twelve output neurons. Including the standard neuron thresholds, the genetic algorithm requires chromosomes with 372 genes. The normal GA-parameters were set as described in section 4.2. The mutation rate is again set to $p_m = 0.6$, and simulations were completed with the crossover rate set to $p_c = 1.0$. The genetic algorithm was run for 1000 generations.

Simulation results

Because of the size of both the training set and the neural network 25 runs have been performed only for the highest crossover rate, each time with different random initialisations (the highest crossover rate of $p_c = 1.0$ has been chosen since this setting has usually given the best results for each crossover type). The graph, showing the results obtained by the various crossover types, is included as figure 5.19.

---

[5] DSTO is the Defence Science and Technology Organisation, located in Salisbury, South Australia.

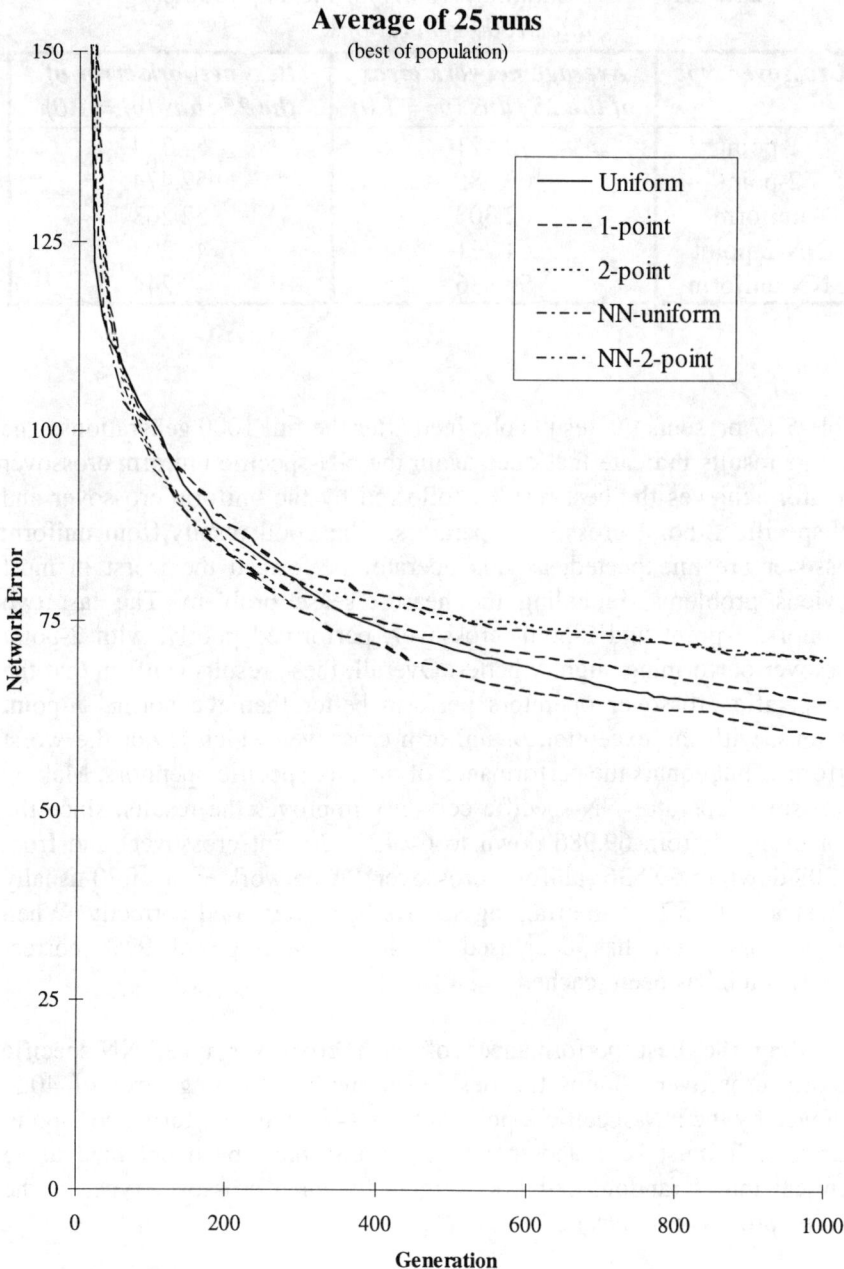

Figure 5.19   *Average results (arithmetic mean) for the ship problem*

Table 5.17   *Simulation results for the ship problem*
after 1000 generations

Crossover type	Average network error of the 25 runs ($p_c = 1.0$)	Best network error of the 25 runs ($p_c = 1.0$)
1-point	70.521	57.344
2-point	69.986	52.474
uniform	62.308	52.263
NN-2-point	64.721	48.293
NN-uniform	59.836	40.244

Table 5.17 presents the results obtained after the full 1000 generations. The average results indicate that once again the NN-specific uniform crossover operator achieves the best results, followed by the uniform crossover and NN-specific 2-point crossover operators. The good results from uniform crossover are unexpected, as this operator performed the worst in most previous problems, including the heart disease problem. The last two operators, 1-point and 2-point crossover, performed poorly, with 2-point crossover performing slightly better. Overall, these results confirm that the NN-specific crossover operators perform better than the normal *n*-point versions, with the exception of uniform crossover which is not the worst performer but equals the performance of the NN-specific operators. Making a crossover operator NN-specific certainly improves the results, since the error dropped from 69.986 down to 64.721 (2-point crossover) and from 62.308 down to 59.836 (uniform crossover). A network error of 70 usually indicates that 95% of the training set has been classified correctly. When the network error has decreased to 40, an average of 97% correct classification has been reached.

Regarding the best performances of each crossover type, NN-specific uniform crossover obtains the best result with a training error of 40.2, followed by the NN-specific 2-point version (48.3), the uniform and 2-point operators. It must be noted that these results have been obtained using identical initial random network weights for each crossover type, as the seeding process is controlled.

5.6 Conclusions

Genetic algorithms rely on 'lucky' random crossovers and mutations, so one method for improving the algorithm was to pursue an increase of the probabilities of success of the crossovers and mutations. The mathematical background, presented in chapter three, provided the basis for the implementation of a neural network specific crossover operator which is based on a reduction of the disruptive character of crossover, preferably while increasing its constructive property. The first goal was achieved by coding the weights of each neuron as neighbouring genes on the chromosomes and subsequently eliminating the potential crossover points within the neuron weight groups. This effectively prevented disruption of successful neurons entirely. By subsequently setting the crossover type to uniform, the construction of effective networks was enhanced. It has been shown that the use of a uniform crossover type also successfully represses the impact of hitch-hikers, which have been known to severely disrupt a fortunate operation of genetic algorithms for problems comparable to neural network weight optimisation. As expected, the results of the case-studies have indicated that this combination of neural network specific uniform crossover indeed provided the best results within any given number of generations.

The mutation operator is the only operator which can introduce new genetic material. Compared to other documented research, the mutation rate was set to a very high value in the simulations performed in this book, and for a good reason: the type of mutation used here is of an entirely different kind than the one which is used in binary genetic algorithms. When mutation is performed in a binary algorithm, it has a very high impact on the chromosome since the gene in question is switched to its opposite state. For real-valued chromosomes however, more graceful mutation operators are available, such as the addition of a probabilistic (e.g. Gaussian) value. This type of mutation has also been used in the experiments in this book. It vastly reduces the impact of mutation and therefore warrants a higher mutation rate. Also, the real-valued coding that was used means that the number of states in which a gene can be, is practically unlimited. This also allows for a much higher mutation rate, as so many more states need to be processed in some way. In conclusion, the mutation operator can be compared to an algorithm such as back-propagation, where many little steps are taken which should ultimately lead towards a solution. This is the task that the mutation operator performs in a genetic algorithm.

6. Comparison of Genetic Algorithms with Back-propagation

This chapter investigates the effectiveness of the usual method of training neural networks: gradient descent learning or, as it is often referred to, back-propagation. The same five problems as in the previous chapter will be used, in order to provide a comparison with the results obtained by the genetic algorithm.

6.1   The back-propagation software

Due to the fact that SUGAL provides a very easy way to perform multiple runs and simultaneously keep a record of several statistical parameters, this programme was also chosen to perform the back-propagation runs. So, as when using the genetic algorithm, each neural network was retained by storing its weights on a chromosome. The population size was determined by the number of runs, for instance if a neural network needed to be trained by back-propagation ten times, each time with random initial weight values, the population size would be set to ten. All weights of each chromosome were randomly initialised in a uniform range between -1 and $+1$, as is common for back-propagation initialisations. By uniformly selecting the two 'parent'-chromosomes, each chromosome would be selected only once to produce 'offspring'. Of course, in this case 'offspring' refers to a 'parent' neural network which has been trained for a number of additional epochs. Since fitness normalisation is not useful, this is set to 'direct' to decrease the amount of time required for the computations. SUGAL always selects two parents (as is natural for a genetic algorithm), which are then passed to the routine performing crossover. Since crossover must not be performed in this case, the crossover rate p_c is set to 0, effectively preventing the two neural networks from being mixed.

The actual back-propagation training is programmed in a new mutation routine, called 'BPlearn', which has been added to the usual SUGAL mutation routines. By setting the mutation rate p_m to 1.0 per chromosome, it has been made certain that this mutation routine was then called upon exactly once for each chromosome, before inserting them in the new population. This replacement is completed 'uniform' and 'unconditional', assuring the newly trained networks do not have to compete with other networks for a place in the new pool. Of course, 'elitism' has been ceased, as this would not only prevent one network from being trained for one generation, but also upset the order of the pool by leaving one parent unselected for training and insertion in the next pool. This chromosome would then be lost forever.

In order to reduce the overhead of the algorithm, it was decided that the mutation operator 'BPlearn' would train a network for fifty epochs before inserting it in the new pool, rendering one generation in SUGAL equal to fifty back-propagation epochs. As implemented, SUGAL performs an effective simultaneous back-propagation learning algorithm for any number of networks and for any number of epochs, while simultaneously collecting statistical information as the minimum and mean network error, and their standard deviation. Out of an initial random pool of networks, all networks are selected in pairs, and are then trained individually and inserted into the pool of the next generation. This is repeated until the desired number of generations (and thus epochs) has been reached. By inspecting the pool, the network error of each individual network can be obtained, providing vital information on the diversity of the final results.

Since it is not within the scope of this investigation to actually optimise the back-propagation algorithm itself, a fixed learning rate of $\varepsilon = 0.5$ was chosen, which is a common setting for smaller problems. Momentum was used only if the normal setting did not obtain satisfactory results. The use of a momentum operator requires the routine to retain the values of the last training step for each network weight. This is no problem during the back-propagation routine itself, but the values do need to be stored between generations. A further difficulty is that the back-propagation routine has no way of tracking chromosomes between generations. These problems can be overcome by doubling the length of each chromosome and storing the values of the last training step in the second half. This has no further effect on the operation of SUGAL, since no other operator makes any changes to the chromosomes. The back-propagation routine with momentum has been programmed as a second new mutation routine, called 'BPmomentum'. When invoked, it recovers the network weight values and the values of the last training step. After the 50 new training steps (with momentum), it stores the new network weights and the new values of the last performed training step back on the chromosome and returns execution to SUGAL.

6.2   Results of the back-propagation training

The set of problems described in the previous chapter were evaluated using the back-propagation learning method. For each problem, the network size was the same as for the genetic algorithms and the same training set was used. The number of epochs for which the networks are trained is set to half the number of evaluations in the genetic algorithm. This compensates for the extra computational effort, necessary after the error evaluation in back-propagation, to propagate the errors back through the network. Since the networks are trained for 50 epochs in each generation, the number of generations required for the back-propagation equals the number of generations for the genetic algorithms, times 50 chromosomes per generations in order to get the number of evaluations, divided by 50 epochs per generation, and finally divided by a half in order to compensate for the extra efforts of back-propagation.

In the following sections, the results for each problem are presented and discussed. Graphs of each problem are included.

The continuous exclusive-OR problem

Since this problem is very small, so 500 runs were performed, each for 6,250 epochs ($\frac{1}{2} \cdot 50 \cdot 250$ generations). Figure 6.1 shows that this problem is on average, easily solved within a thousand epochs or so, where the average network errors drops below a value of one. After steadily reducing the network errors until below 0.1, the speed of optimisation drops, until a final average network error of about $2 \cdot 10^{-3}$ is reached after the 6,250 training epochs. This drop in learning rate is inherent to back-propagation when a sigmoid transfer function is used, as the reduction in network errors forces a reduction in weight changes in future learning steps. Upon inspection of the final population, the smallest network error (best run) was $1.23 \cdot 10^{-3}$, while the largest network error (worst run) was $2.76 \cdot 10^{-3}$. This extremely small spread in the results of the 500 runs strongly indicates that back-propagation experienced no problems in optimising the continuous XOR problem.

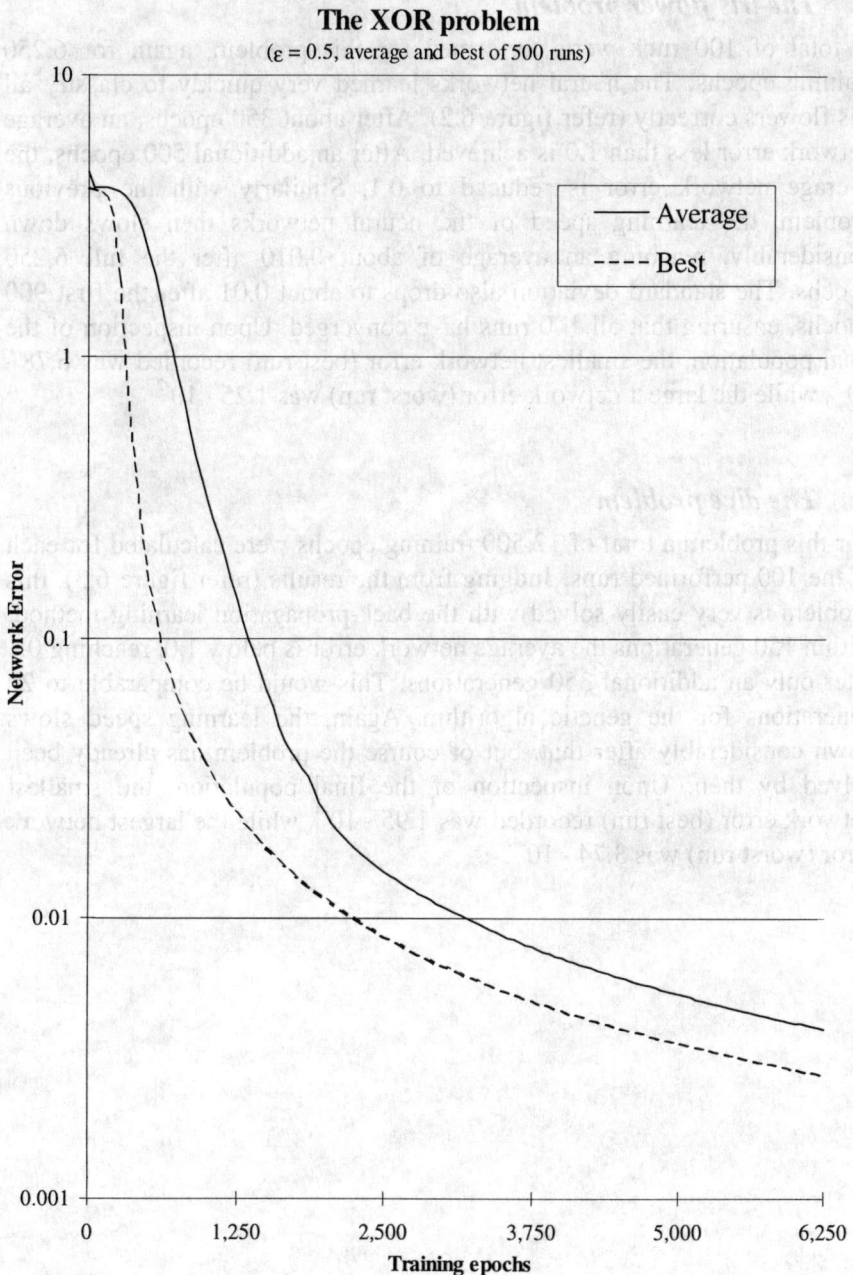

The XOR problem

(ε = 0.5, average and best of 500 runs)

Figure 6.1   Back-propagation results for the continuous XOR problem

The iris flower problem

A total of 100 runs were performed for this problem, again for 6,250 training epochs. The neural networks learned very quickly to classify all iris flowers correctly (refer figure 6.2). After about 350 epochs, an average network error less than 1.0 is achieved. After an additional 500 epochs, the average network error is reduced to 0.1. Similarly with the previous problem, the learning speed of the neural networks then slows down considerably, reaching an average of about 0.010 after the full 6,250 epochs. The standard deviation also drops to about 0.01 after the first 900 epochs, ensuring that all 100 runs have converged. Upon inspection of the final population, the smallest network error (best run) recorded was $6.78 \cdot 10^{-3}$, while the largest network error (worst run) was $1.25 \cdot 10^{-2}$.

The dice problem

For this problem a total of 12,500 training epochs were calculated for each of the 100 performed runs. Judging from the results (refer figure 6.3), this problem is very easily solved with the back-propagation learning method: within 150 generations the average network error is below 1.0, reaching 0.1 after only an additional 350 generations. This would be comparable to 20 generations for the genetic algorithm. Again, the learning speed slows down considerably after that, but of course the problem has already been solved by then. Upon inspection of the final population, the smallest network error (best run) recorded was $1.95 \cdot 10^{-4}$, while the largest network error (worst run) was $3.74 \cdot 10^{-3}$.

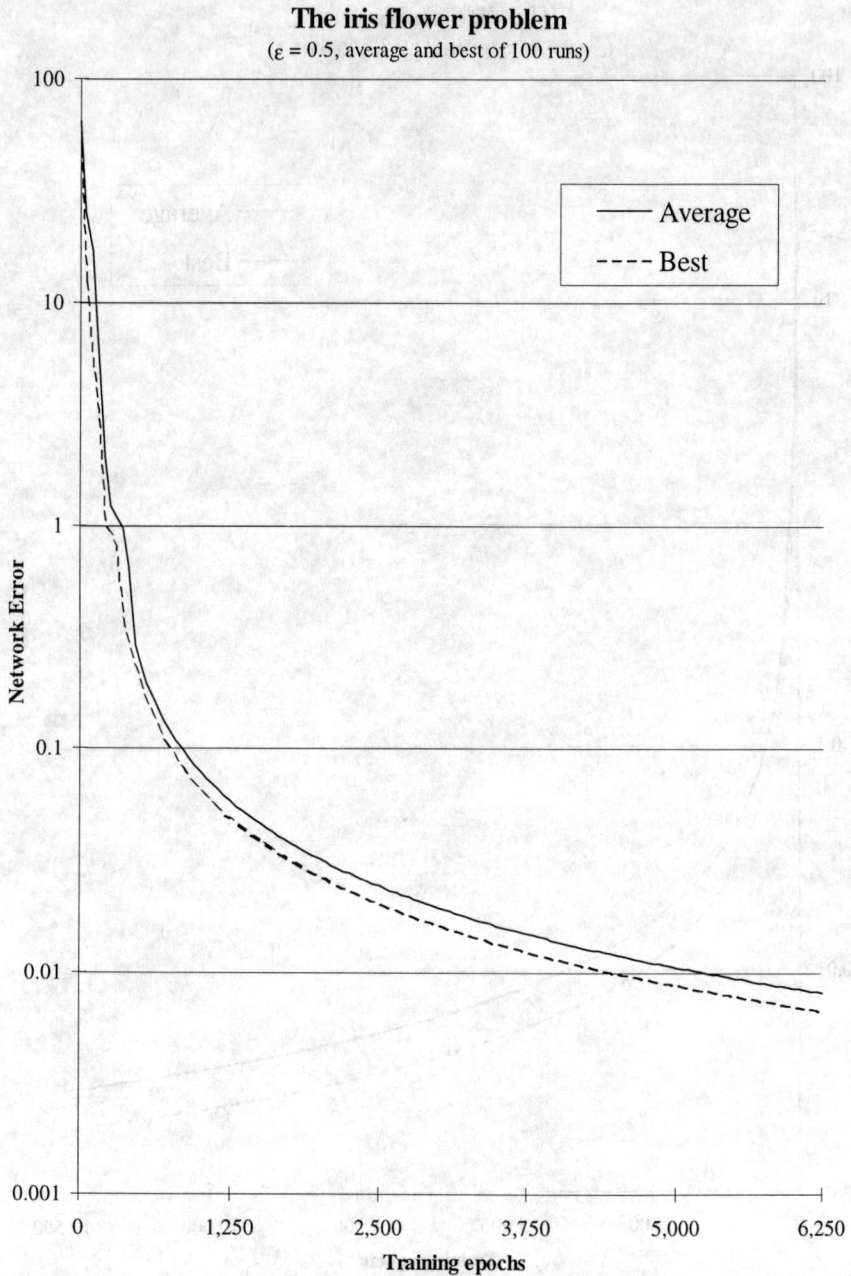

Figure 6.2   *Back-propagation results for the iris flower problem*

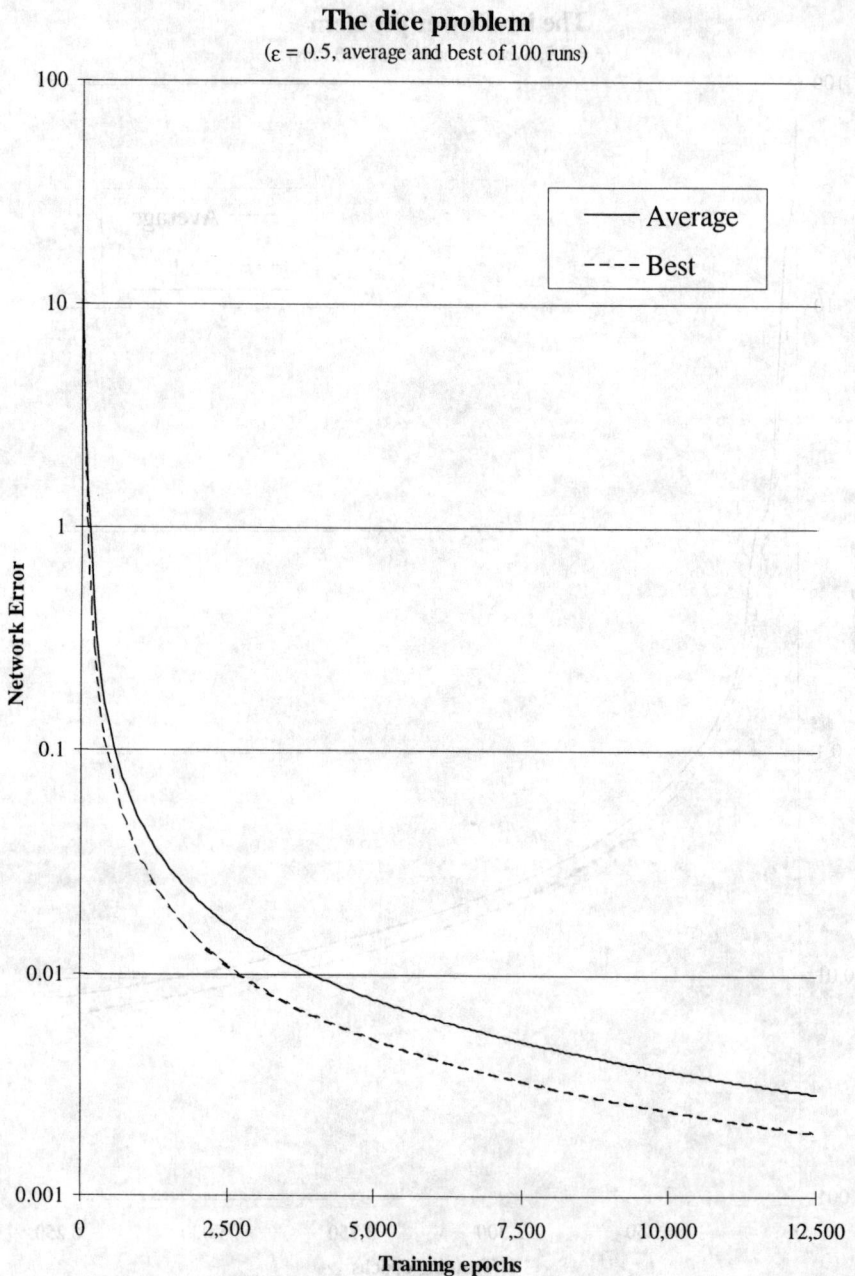

Figure 6.3 *Back-propagation results for the dice problem*

The heart disease problem

For this reasonably complex problem, various settings for the learning rate ε and the momentum rate μ were used: $\varepsilon = 0.5$ with no momentum ($\mu = 0$), $\varepsilon = 0.5$ with momentum $\mu = 0.5$, $\varepsilon = 0.1$ with $\mu = 0.0$, and finally $\varepsilon = 0.1$ with $\mu = 0.5$. For each of these settings 100 runs were performed, during which the networks were trained for 12,500 epochs. Refer table 6.1 for the average and best results of each setting after training had been completed. The full average results are presented in figure 6.4.

Table 6.1	*Results for various settings*	
Setting	*Average result*	*Best result*
$\varepsilon = 0.5, \mu = 0$	3.75	$3.59 \cdot 10^{-3}$
$\varepsilon = 0.5, \mu = 0.5$	7.68	1.01
$\varepsilon = 0.1, \mu = 0.9$	1.71	$1.43 \cdot 10^{-3}$
$\varepsilon = 0.1, \mu = 0.5$	0.44	$9.77 \cdot 10^{-3}$

Clearly, the best results were obtained using the fourth setting ($\varepsilon = 0.1$, $\mu = 0.5$), resulting in an average network error of 0.44 with 74% of the runs reaching a perfect classification of the whole training set. The worst run from the batch using this particular setting halted at an error of 2.51.

The first setting ($\varepsilon = 0.5$, $\mu = 0$) produced only one perfect classification out of the 100 runs performed. Addition of a momentum parameter ($\mu = 5$) produced worse results (refer the second setting of table 6.1). The results for the other settings indicate that the learning rate ε is set too high in the first two cases, making it almost impossible for the back-propagation algorithm to find solutions with low network errors.

When we compare these results with those obtained by the genetic algorithm, the conclusion can be drawn that back-propagation outperforms the genetic algorithm if the right settings for the learning rate ε and momentum rate μ are used. The best solution found by the genetic algorithm still had a network error of 0.891 (NN-specific uniform crossover), after a comparable amount of training. Of course, this is to be expected in view of the more global search technique of the genetic algorithm, when compared to the highly directed search of the gradient descent learning.

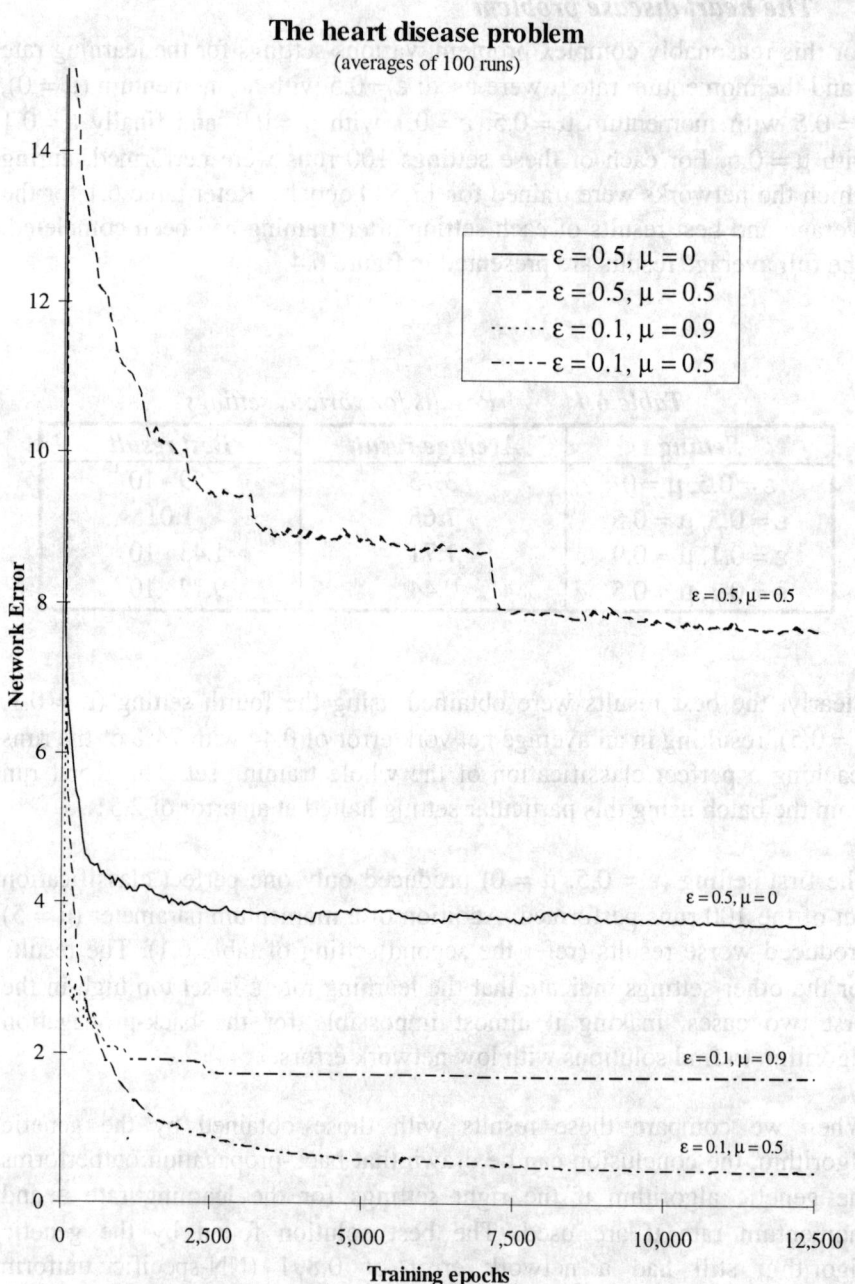

The heart disease problem
(averages of 100 runs)

Figure 6.4   Back-propagation results for the heart disease problem

The ship problem

For this very complex problem, various settings for the learning rate ε and the momentum rate μ were used: $\varepsilon = 0.5$ with no momentum ($\mu = 0$), $\varepsilon = 0.5$ with momentum $\mu = 0.5$, $\varepsilon = 0.3$ with $\mu = 0.5$, $\varepsilon = 0.1$ with $\mu = 0.5$, and finally $\varepsilon = 0.1$ with $\mu = 0.9$. For each of these settings 10 runs are performed, during which the networks were trained for 25,000 epochs. Refer table 6.2 for the average and best results of each setting after training had been completed. The full average results are presented in figure 6.5.

Table 6.2   Results for various settings

Setting	Average result	Best result
$\varepsilon = 0.5, \mu = 0$	78.4	61.0
$\varepsilon = 0.5, \mu = 0.5$	111.4	91.3
$\varepsilon = 0.3, \mu = 0.5$	92.6	61.0
$\varepsilon = 0.1, \mu = 0.5$	18.8	0.026
$\varepsilon = 0.1, \mu = 0.9$	104.7	81.9

Clearly, the best results were obtained using the fourth setting ($\varepsilon = 0.1$, $\mu = 0.5$): an average network error of 18.8 with one run actually reaching a perfect classification of the whole training set. The worst run from the batch using this particular setting ceased learning at an error of 60.0, indicating that success is not guaranteed. An increase of the momentum parameter resulted in even worse results (refer the last setting of table 6.2). The results for the other settings show that the learning parameter ε is also set too high in these cases, making it impossible for the back-propagation algorithm to find solutions with low network errors.

When we compare these results with those obtained by the genetic algorithm, the conclusion can be drawn that back-propagation outperforms the genetic algorithm, if the correct settings for the learning rate ε and momentum rate μ are used. The best solution found by the genetic algorithm still had a network error of 40.2 (NN-specific uniform crossover), after a comparable amount of training.

To test if the genetic algorithm could obtain better results if allowed to operate for more generations, another 10 GA runs were completed. This time, the algorithm was executed for 10,000 generations using NN-specific uniform crossover (same settings as in section 5.5). After the full 10,000 generations, the average network error equalled 34.3, with the best run obtaining a value of 11.1. Although this indicates that the genetic algorithm can reach lower error values, it also shows that it is very slow compared to back-propagation. And even though back-propagation may often find itself stuck in a local optimum if the error space is too complicated, it appears that it is computationally advantageous to perform multiple back-propagation runs rather than a single genetic algorithm run.

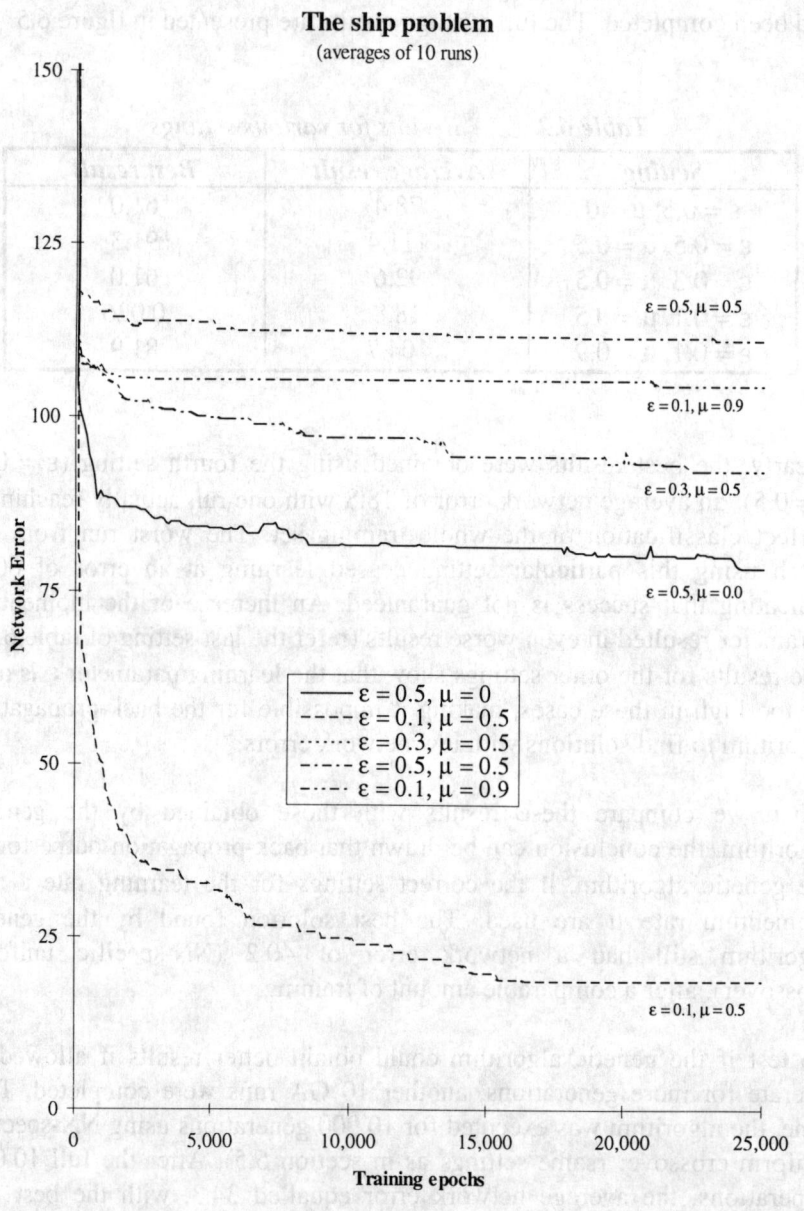

The ship problem

(averages of 10 runs)

Figure 6.5   *Back-propagation results for the ship problem*

6.3   *Conclusions*

For the first three problems, finding a solution presented no difficulty to the genetic algorithm, although back-propagation was faster than the GA. On average, the back-propagation method found a solution about 2.5 times faster than the genetic algorithm for the continuous exclusive OR problem, about 12.5 times faster for the iris flower problem and about 25 times faster for the dice problem. These results can be accounted for by observing the size of the neural network and the complexity of the error landscape. For the genetic algorithm, the length of the chromosomes seems to be the most important factor, since an increase in the number of genes also demands that more genes need to be set to their appropriate values. The correlation between the length of the chromosomes (22, 35 and 102 genes) and the average number of necessary generations (50, 125 and 250 generations respectively), that appears from these three problems supports this. By contrast, back-propagation solves both the iris flower and dice problems within about 500 epochs, however requires an average of about 1,000 epochs for the continuous XOR problem. This suggests the complexity of the error surface is a decisive factor in back-propagation performance, while the actual size of the network is not so important.

The real-life medical heart disease and ship classification problems are much harder to solve. Without the use of momentum, the back-propagation algorithm achieved an average training error of 3.75 for the heart disease problem. The genetic algorithm reached an average of 3.20 with the use of NN-specific uniform crossover. For the ship classification problem, these final network errors were on average 18.8 for back-propagation and 59.8 for the genetic algorithm (again with the use of the NN-specific uniform crossover operator). These network errors correspond to classification rates of about 98.7% and 95.8% respectively. It was also found that the genetic algorithms continue to reduce the errors if allowed to run for more generations. This supports the theory that genetic algorithms are not likely to become stuck in local minimums, as the genetic operators provide a wide search of the problem space. The results from the experiments also support the conclusion that the genetic algorithm can be applied to quite large problems. Perhaps a larger population would be appropriate for the larger problems to compensate for the enormous increase in the number of genes, at the cost of proportionally longer simulation times.

As a general conclusion, it can be said that there is a definite place for the genetic algorithms in neural network training. Further research is required however, in order to make them more competitive with the existing back-propagation methods. For smaller problems without complex error landscapes, back-propagation easily outperforms the genetic algorithm. When the problems become larger and the corresponding error spaces far more complex, back-propagation more often becomes captured in local minimums. This increases the average network error, and allows the genetic algorithm to be somewhat more competitive. However, genetic algorithms are inherently slower, if only since they do not make any use of the available gradient of the error space, as does back-propagation for directing the search.

The primary advantage of the genetic algorithm approach is that it provides a general training mechanism that should be usable for settting weights in a variety of network structures. The application of these techniques to the training of neural networks where back-propagation learning is not appropriate is the next area of research that will be pursued.

References and Further Reading

Antonisse, J., "A New Interpretation of Schema Notation that Overturns the Binary Encoding Constraint", *Proceedings of the Third International Conference on Genetic Algorithms*, Morgan Kaufmann Publishers, pp. 86-91, 1989.

Bridges, C. L., and Goldberg, D. E., "The Nonuniform Walsh-Schema Transform", *Mathematical Foundations of Genetic Algorithms 2*, Morgan Kaufmann Publishers, pp. 13-22, 1993.

Calvin, W. H., "The Emergence of Intelligence", *Scientific American*, special issue on *Life in the Universe*, pp. 79-85, October 1994.

De Jong, K. A., *An Analysis of the Behaviour of a Class of Genetic Adaptive Systems*, Doctoral thesis, Department of Computer and Communication Sciences, University of Michigan, Ann Arbor, 1975.

Eberhart, R. C., "The Role of Genetic Algorithms in Neural Network Query-based Learning and Explanation Facilities", *IEEE International Workshop on Combinations of Genetic Algorithms and Neural Networks (COGANN-92)*, Baltimore, pp. 169-183, 1992.

Eshelman, L. J., and Schaffer, J., D., "Real-Coded Genetic Algorithms and Interval-Schemata", *Mathematical Foundations of Genetic Algorithms 2*, Morgan Kaufmann Publishers, pp. 187-202, 1993.

Forrest, S., and Mitchell, M., "Relative Building-Block Fitness and the Building-Block Hypothesis", *Mathematical Foundations of Genetic Algorithms 2*, Morgan Kaufmann Publishers, pp. 109-126, 1993.

Freeman, J. A., and Skapura, D. M., *Neural Networks, Algorithms, Applications, and Programming Techniques*, Addison-Wesley Publishing Company, 1991.

Goldberg, D. E., *Genetic Algorithms in Search, Optimization & Machine Learning*, Addison-Wesley Publishing Company, 1989.

Grefenstette, J. G., "Deception considered harmful", *Mathematical Foundations of Genetic Algorithms 2*, Morgan Kaufmann Publishers, pp. 75-91, 1993.

Holland, J. H., *Adaptation in Natural and Artificial Systems*, University of Michigan Press, Ann Arbor, 1975.

Jain, L. C. (editor), *Electronic Technology to the year 2000*, IEEE Computer Society Press, USA, 1995.

Janikow, C. Z., and Michalewicz, Z., "An Experimental Comparison of Binary and Floating Point Representations in Genetic Algorithms", *Proceedings of the Fourth International Conference on Genetic Algorithms*, Morgan Kaufman Publishers, pp. 31-36, 1991.

Kitano, H., "Neurogenetic Learning: An Integrated Method of Designing and Training Neural Networks using Genetic Algorithms", *Physica D*, vol. 75, pp. 225-228, 1994.

Kohonen, T., *Self-organization and Associative Memory*, Springer-Verlag, 1984.

Maniezzo, V., "Genetic Evolution of the Topology and Weight Distribution of Neural Networks", *IEEE Transactions on Neural Networks*, Vol. 5, No. 1, 1994.

Montana, D. J., "Automated Parameter Tuning for Interpretation of Synthetic Images", *Handbook of Genetic Algorithms*, van Nostrand Reinhold, pp. 282-331, 1991.

Nelson, M. McCord and Illingworth, W. T., *A Practical Guide to Neural Nets*, Addison-Wesley Publishing Company, 1990.

Spears, W. M., "Crossover or Mutation?", *Mathematical Foundations of Genetic Algorithms 2*, Morgan Kaufmann Publishers, pp. 221-237, 1993.

Spears, W. M., and De Jong, K. A., "An Analysis of Multi-point Crossover", *Foundations of Genetic Algorithms*, Morgan Kaufmann Publishers, pp. 301-315, 1991.

Wright, A. H., "Genetic Algorithms for Real Parameter Optimization", *Foundations of Genetic Algorithms*, Morgan Kaufmann Publishers, pp. 205-218, 1991.

Index